THIS BOOK WILL MAKE YOU RICH GUARANTEED

THE $20 DAILY INVESTMENT WEALTH PROMISE

Justice S.M. Prosperity

Desclaimer

The information contained in this book is provided for **educational and informational purposes only** and should not be construed as financial, investment, tax, legal, or other professional advice.

While every effort has been made to ensure the accuracy of the information presented, the author and publisher make no guarantees regarding the results that may be obtained from the use of this material. **Past performance does not guarantee future results.** All investing involves risk, including the potential loss of principal.

Readers are encouraged to **consult with licensed financial advisors, legal counsel, tax professionals, or other qualified professionals** before making any financial decisions. The examples, strategies, and projections in this book are based on general circumstances and may not apply to your individual situation.

The author and publisher shall not be held liable for any loss or damage resulting from any action taken or reliance made by any person on the information contained in this publication.

Use this material as a guide—not a guarantee. Always do your own research and exercise wisdom.

Preface

We live in a time when the dream of financial freedom feels increasingly out of reach for many. Skyrocketing costs, stagnant wages, and economic uncertainty have left countless individuals wondering if they will ever achieve lasting wealth or security. Yet, in the midst of this uncertainty, there remains a powerful truth: small, consistent actions, guided by faith and strategy, can yield extraordinary results over time.

This book was born out of that truth.

THIS BOOK WILL MAKE YOU RICH GUARANTEED chronicles the inspiring journey of three ordinary friends who refused to let their circumstances dictate their destiny. Instead of waiting for perfect conditions or large windfalls, they embraced a bold yet simple plan—invest $20 a day, buy rental properties annually, and reinvest their earnings with discipline and vision.

Their story is not built on speculation or get-rich-quick schemes. It's grounded in practical steps, sound financial principles, and the power of compound growth. It shows how leveraging home equity, embracing delayed gratification, and committing to long-term goals can turn modest savings into a multi-million-dollar real estate portfolio.

This book is more than a financial playbook—it's a testimony to what's possible when ordinary people unite with a common vision, take consistent action, and trust the process. Whether you're a beginner with limited capital, a working professional looking for a side investment, or someone simply seeking inspiration to begin your wealth-building journey, this book will empower you with the tools, mindset, and strategy to build lasting prosperity.

You don't need to be wealthy to start. But you must start to become wealthy.

Welcome to your journey toward financial freedom—one daily decision at a time.

Forward

What if I told you that greatness doesn't begin with money — it begins with mindset? That becoming wealthy isn't about winning the lottery or having a genius IQ — it's about making one small, powerful decision... every single day.This book you're holding isn't just about real estate or saving money. It's a guide to rewiring the way you think about success, discipline, and your future. It's a revolution in $20-a-day steps. Three ordinary friends didn't wait for a perfect moment or a million-dollar idea. They chose to start small, stay consistent, and walk together toward a vision bigger than themselves. That's what makes this book special. Because if they can do it — you can too. You may be a teenager reading this, wondering how your $5 allowance or part-time job could ever turn into something big. Or maybe you're an adult with responsibilities and regrets, feeling like you've missed your chance. Let me tell you: You haven't. Wealth isn't reserved for the lucky. It's reserved for the disciplined. The determined. The ones who are willing to believe before they see. Inside these pages, you'll learn the real secrets:

- How to escape the traps that keep most people poor
- How to turn a daily habit into a lifelong fortune
- How to think, pray, and act like someone destined to prosper.

This book won't just change your finances. It will challenge your mindset. It will stretch your faith. It will ignite your purpose. So take a deep breath. Read with expectation. And remember greatness is never out of reach for those who dare to begin. Let this be the book that changes everything

. — JUSTICE S.M. PROSPERITY (Bsc, MS, MHA, MBA, DBA (c) PTP)

Visionary| Entrepreneur | Financial and Investment Strategist| Financial Apostle General| Kingdom Financier| Author

Reader Testimonials

"This chapter changed how I see money forever. I never imagined $20 a day could become millions until now. It gave me hope and a real plan." – ***Aisha M., 19-year-old student***

"I've read countless finance books, but this one made me pause. It's simple, powerful, and unforgettable. This is the blueprint for financial freedom." – ***James R., Entrepreneur***

"As a single mom, I never thought investing was within my reach. After reading this, I opened my first savings account and set a goal to buy my first home." – ***Leticia G., Nurse and Mother of Two***

"This chapter is not just inspiring—it's life-changing. I wish I had this 10 years ago. Every teenager in America should read this." – ***Terrence B., High School Teacher***

"It's mind-blowing how simple and practical this strategy is. This isn't theory—it's a real story with real numbers and a real future." – ***Remi D., IT Consultant***

"What I loved most is that it made me believe I can do it too. You don't need to be rich. You just need to start." – ***Maria K., College Freshman***

"This isn't a book—it's a movement. Every young person deserves to know how powerful daily habits can be." – ***Chidi A., Youth Pastor***

"I shared this chapter with my teenage son and daughter. For the first time, they're excited about investing and saving!" – ***Jennifer T., Financial Coach***

"The way this chapter blends faith, strategy, and real estate is genius. It's proof that God can multiply even the smallest seed." – ***Justin P., Minister and Investor***

"I've been in real estate for years, and this reminded me why I started. The simplicity of this plan makes it foolproof—and powerful." – ***Lue M., Real Estate Agent***

About the Author

Justice S.M. Prosperity (BSc, MS, MHA, MBA, DBA(c), PTP) is more than a name—it is a mantle, a mission, and a movement. He is a Visionary, Entrepreneur, Financial and Investment Strategist, Personal Finance Authority, Financial Apostle General, Kingdom Financier and a bestselling author

Renowned as a dynamic speaker, visionary entrepreneur, ordained minister, and financial strategist, Justice is a rare voice that bridges two worlds: **faith and finance**. Whether in corporate boardrooms or church pulpits, his words electrify, educate, and empower. With every message, he helps people not just survive—but rise, rebuild, and rule during even the most turbulent economic seasons.

Over the last decade, Justice has emerged as a **trailblazing authority in financial empowerment and strategic wealth-building**. He has guided many companies, small business owners, investors, and working families through complex challenges—from global supply chain disruptions to personal financial crises—always delivering clarity, courage, and concrete results.

As Founder and CEO of *Tax and Bookkeeping Done Right LLC*, he equips individuals and organizations to master their money, minimize tax burdens, and build sustainable, generational wealth. His revolutionary approach—where **biblical wisdom meets financial precision**—has earned him the title: **"The Financial Apostle."** He is a bold bridge between eternal truths and economic transformation.

Justice's academic credentials are as impressive as his impact. He holds three master's degrees:

- Mechanical Engineering from Tuskegee University

- Health Administration from St. Joseph's University
- MBA in Finance from Fayetteville State University

He is currently completing his **Doctorate in Business Administration (DBA)** at Liberty University—an embodiment of his relentless pursuit of mastery and meaning.

As a bestselling author, Justice has written game-changing books such as *Answers to Your Money Problems, This Book Will Make You Rich,* and *Tariffs, Trade Wars and Your Wallet, From $20 to Millions,* Each one is a blueprint for financial freedom, challenging systems of scarcity and igniting a new generation of wise stewards.

Yet beyond accolades and academic degrees, what sets Justice apart is his **lived experience**. He's a father, an investor, a business owner, and a man of unshakable faith. He has faced economic storms and spiritual battles—and emerged with divine strategy in hand.

Through this book, Justice continues his mission:

To **awaken destinies**,

break financial bondage,

and **raise up leaders** who prosper not just with money, but with mission and meaning.

Because as he often teaches:

True wealth begins with wisdom.

Abundance flows through alignment.

And **lasting success is born from living with divine intention.**

Disclaimer: This book will teach you to be rich if you apply and commit yourself to every single principle advocated for in this book. It requires 100% verifiable commitment.

Contact: ***832 543 3178***

EMAIL: **prosperitypath77@gmail.com**

Opening Prayer

Heavenly Father,

Thank You for this moment, for this book, and for the opportunity to grow—in wisdom, in faith, and in purpose. Lord, as I begin this journey, open my heart and mind to see the possibilities You've already placed in my hands. Help me to understand that wealth is not just about money, but about stewardship, obedience, and vision.

Break every limiting belief that says, "I can't," "I'm too late," or "I'm not enough." Replace fear with faith, and replace doubt with discipline. Teach me to value the small things, the daily seeds, and the quiet steps that lead to abundance.

Let this book be more than information—let it be transformation. Let it awaken something deep inside me that dares to dream bigger, plan smarter, and believe that with You, all things are possible.

Bless the author, the readers, and everyone who will be inspired to take action. Multiply the impact of these pages, and use them to raise up a new generation of faithful stewards, purpose-driven investors, and wealth-builders with kingdom mindsets.

In Jesus' mighty name I pray,Amen.

Contents

Chapter 1

From $20 a Day to Millions

A Real Estate Wealth Journey

In a world where financial freedom often feels like a distant dream, three friends made a bold commitment to prove otherwise. Armed with vision, discipline, and a simple strategy, they transformed small daily savings into a real estate empire worth millions. This chapter tells their inspiring journey—how consistent investing, leveraging equity, and long-term thinking turned $20 a day into generational wealth.

The Foundation: Year 1–5

The journey began with each friend contributing a one-time initial amount of $7,000, pooled together to meet the 8% down payment on their first $200,000 rental property. Rather than wait for large windfalls, they committed to saving $20 per day per person—totaling $21,900 annually.

Over the first five years, they followed a straightforward plan: acquire one new property annually using their savings for the down payment. By Year 5, they had secured five rental homes, each generating $14,000 in annual rental income. Their combined annual cash flow stood at $70,000. With steady home appreciation at 7% per year and ongoing mortgage paydown, their net worth grew to approximately $218,417.

This phase showcased the power of consistency and teamwork. They didn't chase risky deals or speculative flips—instead, they built patiently and deliberately.

Strategic Acceleration: Year 6–10

In Year 6, a strategic shift occurred. They tapped into the equity accumulated in their first property—approximately $21,000—and used it as a second down payment. This enabled them to purchase two properties instead of one, using their regular annual savings alongside the equity.

From that point forward, they continued this cycle: withdrawing $21,000 of equity from a property purchased five years earlier and combining it with their current savings to buy two homes annually. This technique, known as equity recycling, allowed them to accelerate acquisitions while minimizing new debt exposure.

By Year 10, they had amassed 15 rental properties. Their annual rental income had surged to $210,000, and their estimated net worth had climbed to $1,317,472. The snowball was now rolling.

Momentum and Expansion: Year 11–15

By the midpoint of their 20-year plan, the friends' portfolio had grown significantly. Thanks to their continued strategy of equity extraction and reinvestment, they reached 25 properties by Year 15. The compounding effects of real estate investing—appreciation, rental income, and mortgage paydown—were now fully evident.

Their annual rental cash flow hit $350,000, and their net worth exceeded $3.42 million. What started as a humble effort among friends had become a wealth-building machine. The consistency of savings and the discipline to reinvest earnings helped them maintain momentum.

Financial Freedom Realized: Year 16–20

In the final stretch of the 20-year plan, the friends reached a major milestone: 35 rental homes. These properties, appreciating in value at 7% per year and producing steady rental income, generated $490,000 annually. Their estimated net worth surpassed $6.85 million.

Their journey revealed the true power of leveraged growth. Every home not only paid for itself through rental income but also became a building block for acquiring the next. Through careful financial planning, risk management, and long-term commitment, the trio turned a simple daily habit into financial freedom.

Reflections and Lessons Learned

- Small Habits, Big Impact: Saving $20 a day seemed insignificant at first, but over time, it became the fuel for a multi-million dollar portfolio.- Teamwork Multiplies Results: By pooling resources and making joint decisions, the friends accelerated progress far beyond what each could do alone.- Equity is a Wealth Lever: Strategic use of equity from appreciating assets enabled them to grow their holdings without needing external investors or massive capital injections.- Time is the Greatest Ally: The compounding effects of real estate become exponential with time. The longer the investment horizon, the greater the rewards.

Conclusion

This chapter is not just about real estate. It's about belief, discipline, and the power of a simple plan executed faithfully over time. These three friends started with an ordinary idea, acted on it daily, and built extraordinary wealth. Anyone can follow this blueprint—with vision, commitment, and the willingness to begin today.

Chapter 2

Setting the Stage

Dreams of an Empire

In the world of real estate, the dreams of building an empire often seem reserved for those with deep pockets or advanced degrees. However, the story of three friends who embarked on their journey with just twenty dollars a day proves that passion, creativity, and teamwork can turn a simple idea into a thriving venture. This book will take you on their inspiring journey, demonstrating that anyone, even teenagers with a shared vision, can navigate the exciting yet challenging realm of real estate investing. Here, we will explore how they transformed their modest resources into a flourishing business, one step at a time.

Starting with just twenty dollars a day, these friends discovered that every penny could be maximized through thoughtful budgeting and collaboration. They pooled their resources, shared their dreams, and supported each other through the ups and downs of their journey. This collaborative spirit not only strengthened their friendship but also taught them vital lessons about cooperative investment strategies. By leveraging each other's strengths and skills, they learned that real estate investing is not solely about finances, but also about building trust and fostering relationships, both with each other and within the community.

As they ventured deeper into the world of real estate, they encountered various creative financing methods that allowed them to stretch their limited budget further. From exploring unconventional loans to utilizing grants and partnerships, they became adept at thinking outside the box. This book will introduce you to these innovative financing techniques and how they can empower you to take your first steps into real estate, even if you're starting from scratch. The friends' journey emphasizes that with determination and resourcefulness, financial barriers can be overcome.

In addition to financing, the friends learned valuable lessons about low-cost property management techniques. They discovered that effective management doesn't require a huge budget but rather a willingness to learn, adapt, and be proactive. By sharing responsibilities and dividing tasks based on individual strengths, they maximized their efficiency and minimized costs. This book will provide you with practical tips and strategies to manage properties on a budget, showing that intelligent management can lead to greater success and satisfaction in your investments.

Finally, the friends recognized the importance of building a real estate network on a budget. They attended local meetups, engaged with mentors, and learned from seasoned investors who were willing to share their knowledge. By establishing connections within their community, they opened doors to new opportunities and resources. This book will guide you through the process of networking effectively, emphasizing that relationships are just as crucial as capital in the world of real estate. Your dream of building an empire is not just about money; it's about the connections you forge and the support you cultivate along the way.

Chapter 3

Personal Credit and Real Estate

Mastering Personal Credit with Real Estate

1. What Is Personal Credit?

Personal credit is your financial reputation. It tells lenders, landlords, and financial institutions how trustworthy you are with borrowed money. Think of it as your adult financial report card. Your credit is built on your history of paying back debt—credit cards, loans, utility bills, and even some subscriptions. The higher your credit score, the more opportunities you unlock: lower interest rates, better loan terms, higher borrowing limits, and—most importantly—access to funding for real estate acquisition and wealth building.

2. How to Establish Credit if You Don't Have One

If you've never taken out a loan or used a credit card, you may not have a credit score. But no worries—everyone starts somewhere. Here's how to get started:

- Apply for a secured credit card
- Become an authorized user on someone else's account
- Use credit-building loans from local credit unions
- Report rent and utility payments using services like Experian Boost

Action Step: Start small. Set up one or two credit-building accounts and pay them like clockwork. Automate payments to avoid late fees.

3. How to Fix Bad Credit

If your credit is damaged by missed payments, defaults, or collections, don't panic—bad credit isn't permanent. With the right strategy, it can be repaired and transformed.

- Check your credit report from AnnualCreditReport.com
- Dispute inaccuracies with credit bureaus
- Catch up on past-due accounts
- Negotiate with creditors for better terms or deletions
- Reduce credit utilization below 30% (ideally under 10%)
- Avoid applying for unnecessary credit

4. How to Improve Your Credit Score

Improving your score takes consistency and time. Always pay on time, keep older accounts open, maintain a diverse mix of credit, and minimize hard inquiries.

5. Leveraging Credit to Buy Residential Property

Good credit opens doors in real estate. A high score means lower interest rates and better mortgage terms. It also increases your chance of approval for loans like FHA or DSCR loans, business lines of credit, and HELOCs.

6. Using Credit for Real Estate Accumulation

With strong credit, you can strategically grow your property portfolio. Start with a low-down-payment loan, build equity, and use HELOCs or cash-out refinances to fund new purchases. Rinse and repeat.

7. Final Thoughts: Turn Credit Into Capital

Your credit score is not just a number—it's a financial passport. Treat it as a dynamic asset you can grow and use to create a real estate empire. The journey starts with knowledge and commitment.

Chapter 4

What is Real Estate Investing

The Basics

Understanding the basics of real estate investing is the first step towards building your own empire, especially when you're just starting with a small budget. Imagine pooling together your resources with friends to explore investment opportunities that may seem out of reach for most teenagers. With just twenty dollars a day, you can embark on a journey that not only teaches you about finances but also strengthens your friendships. The world of real estate is vast, and with the right mindset and determination, you can turn your dreams into reality, one property at a time.

Real estate investing is not just for seasoned professionals; anyone with a passion for learning can enter this exciting field. The key is to start small and grow gradually. By investing together with friends, you can share the financial burden and responsibilities. Think of it as a team sport where each member contributes their skills and ideas. By pooling your resources, you can access properties that would typically be out of your financial reach. This cooperative strategy not only minimizes risk but also enhances the learning experience as you navigate the complexities of the market together.

Creative financing methods are critical when you're working with limited funds. Traditional loans may not be feasible for teenagers, but there are alternatives. Consider options like seller financing, where the property owner allows you to pay them directly over time. You might also look into crowdfunding platforms that enable groups to invest in real estate projects. These methods empower you to think outside the box and develop innovative solutions to financial challenges. Remember, ingenuity is often more valuable than a hefty bank account when it comes to real estate.

Managing properties doesn't have to break the bank either. Many low-cost property management techniques can help you maintain your investments without overwhelming expenses. From DIY repairs to utilizing free online resources for tenant screening, you can learn to manage properties effectively while keeping costs low. Embrace the idea that every challenge is an opportunity to learn. By taking on management tasks together, you not only save money but also foster a sense of shared responsibility and teamwork among friends.

Building a real estate network on a budget is essential for long-term success. Attend local meetups, join online forums, and leverage social media to connect with other investors and mentors. Networking can lead to valuable partnerships, knowledge, and even potential deals. Don't be afraid to approach experienced investors; many are willing to share insights and guidance. By surrounding yourself with supportive individuals who share your passion, you can gain confidence and inspiration as you embark on your real estate journey. Remember, every big dream starts with a small step, and with the right mindset, your twenty bucks can lead to something extraordinary.

Chapter 5
The Dream Begins
Discovering the Power of Dreams

Discovering the power of dreams is the first step on an incredible journey into the world of real estate. Imagine waking up every morning with a clear vision of what you want to achieve. Dreams aren't just fantasies; they can be powerful motivators that drive you toward your goals. Whether it's owning a multi-family home, starting a property management business, or creating a community of affordable housing, these dreams can shape your path. When three friends come together with just twenty bucks a day, they prove that even the wildest aspirations can come to life with determination and teamwork.

The beauty of dreams is that they can evolve. When you first start your journey in real estate, your vision might be small, like renting out a room in your house or flipping a budget-friendly property. As you gain knowledge and experience, those dreams can expand. You might find yourself dreaming about owning several properties, forming partnerships with other investors, or even creating a real estate network that supports others in your community. By nurturing your dreams and allowing them to grow, you can create a roadmap for your future that is not only achievable but also inspiring to others around you.

Real estate is a unique field where creativity can flourish. It is essential to dream big but also to think outside the box when it comes to financing and investment strategies. With just twenty bucks a day, your group can explore cooperative investment strategies that allow everyone to contribute while minimizing individual risk. You can pool your resources, share ideas, and collaborate on projects that align with your collective dreams. This approach not only makes real estate investing more accessible but also strengthens the bonds of friendship as you work together toward a common goal.

As you embark on this adventure, remember that every successful investor started as a beginner. Embrace the learning process and allow your dreams to guide you. Seek out low-cost property management techniques that fit your budget and learn how to house hack for group investments. By turning your living space into a source of income, you can accelerate your journey toward financial independence. Each step you take will be fueled by the vision you hold in your heart, transforming challenges into opportunities.

Ultimately, discovering the power of dreams is about taking that first leap of faith. Encourage one another to keep dreaming, even when the path seems uncertain. Your combined aspirations can lead to amazing possibilities, and as you build your real estate empire, remember that each property bought and every dollar saved is a testament to your hard work and dedication. Together, you can turn twenty bucks a day into a legacy that inspires others to believe in the power of their dreams.

Meeting My Future Partners

Meeting my future partners was a pivotal moment in my journey toward building our real estate empire. It wasn't just about finding people who shared a common interest in real estate; it was about discovering friends who embodied the same passion, ambition, and vision for the future. We were all teenagers, navigating the complexities of life, yet united by a singular dream: to invest in real estate despite our limited resources. The challenge ahead was daunting, but I realized that with the right people by my side, we could turn our twenty bucks a day into something extraordinary.

Our first meetings were casual, filled with excitement and brainstorming sessions. We gathered in basements, coffee shops, and parks, discussing our dreams and the strategies we could employ to make them come true. Each friend brought unique strengths to the table. Some were natural negotiators, others had a knack for research, and a few possessed an uncanny ability to think creatively. This diversity became our greatest asset. By pooling our talents, we could tackle challenges that seemed insurmountable on our own. We quickly learned that real estate wasn't just about money; it was about leveraging our collective skills to identify opportunities and navigate obstacles.

As we began to explore the world of real estate investing, we realized that building a network was essential. We reached out to local real estate groups, joined online forums, and attended workshops. Each interaction introduced us to seasoned investors who were eager to share their knowledge and experiences. These mentors became invaluable resources, guiding us through the intricacies of budget real estate investing. They taught us about creative financing methods, cooperative investment strategies, and the significance of house hacking, all of which were crucial for us as young, aspiring investors with limited funds.

One of the most exhilarating aspects of our journey was discovering low-cost property management techniques. We knew we couldn't afford to hire professionals, so we took it upon ourselves to learn the ropes. From managing tenants to maintaining properties, we split responsibilities based on our strengths. This hands-on approach not only kept our expenses low but also strengthened our bond as partners. We celebrated our wins together and learned from our mistakes, each experience molding us into more knowledgeable investors. The camaraderie we built during these times became the foundation of our partnership.

Meeting my future partners transformed my outlook on what was possible. Together, we were not just three teens with a dream; we were a team determined to create a real estate empire from the ground up. Our journey taught us that success is not solely about financial investment but about investing in relationships and learning from one another. As we continue to chase our dreams, I am inspired by the thought that with determination and collaboration, anyone can turn a mere twenty bucks a day into a thriving venture. Our story is just beginning, and the possibilities are endless.

The $20 Challenge

The $20 Challenge is an exciting journey into the world of real estate, designed specifically for you and your friends to explore the possibilities of building wealth together. Imagine pooling your resources with just twenty bucks a day, transforming that modest amount into a thriving real estate empire. This challenge is not only about money; it's about creativity, teamwork, and learning how to leverage limited resources to achieve something extraordinary. By taking on this challenge, you'll discover that investing in real estate doesn't have to be daunting or reserved for the wealthy.

When you start the $20 Challenge, the first step is to gather your friends and set a clear goal. Decide what you want to achieve together, whether it's purchasing your first rental property, flipping houses, or even investing in real estate crowdfunding opportunities. With collective ambition, you can brainstorm innovative ideas on how to use your daily budget effectively. Each member can contribute their unique skills and perspectives, creating a dynamic environment where everyone feels empowered to share and grow. Remember, collaboration is key, and the more ideas you generate, the better your chances of success.

As you embark on this adventure, you'll quickly learn about budget real estate investing. It's important to research newly built and find hidden gems in your area. Utilize online resources, local classifieds, and even word-of-mouth to discover potential investments that fit your budget. The $20 Challenge encourages you to think outside the box and consider unconventional properties that may not be on everyone's radar. By pooling your knowledge and resources, you can identify opportunities that others might overlook, helping you maximize your investment potential.

Cooperative investment strategies are at the heart of the $20 Challenge. You and your friends can create a mini real estate investment group, where each person invests their daily contribution into a shared fund. This not only helps you accumulate capital faster but also teaches you about shared decision-making and responsibility. As a team, you'll learn to analyze properties, negotiate deals, and even manage your investments together. This experience will not only build your financial literacy but also strengthen your friendships as you navigate the ups and downs of real estate investing side by side.

Lastly, embrace the spirit of house hacking and creative financing methods. House hacking allows you to live in a property while renting out rooms, helping you pay your mortgage and build equity simultaneously. With the $20 Challenge, you can explore creative financing options such as seller financing or partnerships with local investors. These strategies can open doors that traditional financing might close. By thinking creatively and working together, you'll not only achieve your real estate dreams but also learn valuable life skills that will serve you well beyond the challenge. So gather your friends, take that first step, and let the $20 Challenge lead you on an incredible journey toward financial independence and friendship

Chapter 6

The Case for New Homes

Why Buying a New Home Beats Buying Used

When it comes to building wealth through real estate, one of the most important decisions is whether to buy new construction or a resale (used) home. While both can be viable, this chapter lays out why, in many cases, buying a new home offers greater financial benefits, fewer headaches, and more long-term value—especially for investors and first-time buyers. Let's break it down.

1. Builder Incentives: Free Money on the Table

Unlike resale homes, new home builders are highly motivated to close deals quickly. Why? Because their business depends on volume and market absorption. To sweeten the deal, many builders offer substantial incentives, including:

- Down payment assistance
- Closing cost coverage
- Interest rate buy-downs or mortgage rate locks
- Free or upgraded appliances and fixtures
- Home warranty

These are offers you'll rarely find when buying a used home—and they can easily add $20,000–$40,000 in total value to your purchase.

2. No Repairs or Renovations Needed

Used homes often come with outdated systems or hidden surprises. New homes? They're move-in ready, code-compliant, energy-efficient, and less likely to need repairs for years.

3. Energy Efficiency

= Lower Monthly Costs New homes are built with better insulation, appliances, and smart HVAC systems—resulting in significantly lower utility bills.

4. Safety, Technology & Smart Design

New homes include modern safety standards, smart tech, and optimized layouts designed for today's lifestyle needs.

5. Better Financing Options

Builders partner with preferred lenders to offer exclusive mortgage deals, often reducing fees, interest rates, and approval barriers.

6. Easier Resale & Higher Renter Appeal

New homes appreciate faster and rent easier due to lower maintenance needs and more modern appeal

When Might a Used Home Be Better?

Used homes may be preferable for fix-and-flip strategies, unique properties, or mature neighborhoods with character—but they often come with risks and renovation costs. The Bottom Line. New homes are strategic assets offering builder incentives, savings, efficiency, and appreciation potential—especially when paired with disciplined investing.

Reflection:

Choose Assets, Not Headaches When building your real estate empire, choose assets that grow, last, and simplify your journey. A new home isn't just a purchase—it's a launchpad.

Chapter 7
Understanding Real Estate

What is Real Estate?

Real estate is more than just buildings and land; it's a powerful avenue for creating wealth and making dreams come true. Imagine a place where you and your friends can come together, pooling your resources and creativity to invest in properties that can generate income and build your future. Real estate is about recognizing the potential in a piece of land or a house and transforming that potential into something greater. It's the excitement of finding a hidden gem, the thrill of negotiation, and the satisfaction of seeing your investment grow over time.

At its core, real estate involves buying, selling, or leasing properties, whether they are homes, commercial spaces, or vacant land. For teenagers, this might seem like a distant goal, but the reality is that you can start small. With just a little bit of money—think about those twenty bucks you spend every day—you can learn the ropes of real estate investing. The key is understanding that every great empire starts with a single step. By educating yourselves about the market, seeking out deals, and collaborating with friends, you can turn your small investments into something significant.

Cooperative investment strategies are where the magic happens. Imagine you and your friends each contributing a small amount of money toward a shared goal. This teamwork allows you to pool your resources, making it easier to purchase properties that would be out of reach individually. By working together, you not only share the financial burden but also the knowledge and skills that come with each investment. This creates a supportive environment where everyone learns and grows, transforming the daunting world of real estate into an accessible and exciting adventure.

Creative financing methods play a crucial role in making real estate investing achievable, even on a tight budget. You don't need to have a mountain of cash to start; instead, think outside the box. Options like seller financing, lease options, or even partnerships can open doors that you never thought possible. These methods allow you to acquire properties with little to no upfront costs, enabling you to focus on building your portfolio. With imagination and determination, you can find ways to invest without breaking the bank, proving that financial limitations can be overcome with clever strategies.

Lastly, building a real estate network on a budget is essential for your success. Surrounding yourself with like-minded individuals who share your passion for real estate can lead to new opportunities and valuable insights. Attend local meetups, join online forums, or even create your own group of aspiring investors. Engaging with others will not only motivate you but also provide resources and knowledge that can accelerate your journey. By nurturing these relationships, you'll foster a community that supports each other in reaching your dreams, proving that together, you can achieve more than you ever could alone.

Why Real Estate is a Smart Investment

Real estate is often seen as a realm reserved for the wealthy, but the truth is, it can be a smart investment for anyone, including teenagers just starting out. Imagine pooling together just twenty bucks a day with your friends to create something incredible. Real estate offers the chance to build wealth, learn valuable skills, and even create a lasting legacy. When you dive into the world of property investment, you're not just buying a piece of land or a building; you're investing in your future and the dreams you share with your friends.

One of the most compelling reasons to consider real estate is its potential for appreciation. Over time, property values tend to rise, meaning that what you buy today could be worth much more tomorrow. By working together with your friends, you can leverage your limited resources to purchase properties that might otherwise be out of reach. This collective effort not only makes investing more accessible but also amplifies your potential gains. You're not just making a purchase; you're embarking on a journey toward financial independence.

Budget real estate investing is all about being smart with your money. It teaches you to prioritize your spending and think creatively about how to maximize every dollar. By learning to invest on a budget, you can discover low-cost strategies that make real estate accessible. Whether it's through house hacking—living in one part of a multi-family property while renting out the others—or utilizing cooperative investment strategies, you and your friends can find ways to make your money work harder for you. These methods allow you to enter the real estate market without breaking the bank, proving that every little bit counts.

The power of networking cannot be underestimated in real estate. As teenagers, you have the unique opportunity to build relationships early on that can support your investment goals. By connecting with mentors, local investors, and other young entrepreneurs, you can gain insights, advice, and even partnership opportunities that will benefit your journey. Your network can help you learn about creative financing methods, uncover hidden deals, and share tips on effective property management. Building a network on a budget means you can access resources and knowledge without significant financial investment, making your real estate dreams more attainable.

In the end, investing in real estate with your friends is about more than just money; it's about teamwork, learning, and growth. Each step you take together teaches you valuable lessons about responsibility, collaboration, and innovative thinking. As you navigate challenges and celebrate successes, you will grow stronger as individuals and as a team. Remember, every empire starts with a single step. With just twenty bucks a day and the support of your friends, you can build a real estate empire that not only changes your financial future but also enriches your lives in ways you never imagined.

The Basics of Buying Properties

The journey of buying properties begins with understanding the basics. For teenagers eager to dive into the world of real estate, it's essential to grasp the core principles that guide successful property purchases. Real estate is not just about the money; it's about vision, teamwork, and the drive to turn a small investment into something monumental. With just twenty bucks a day, you and your friends can start laying the groundwork for your very own real estate empire, one property at a time.

First, research is your best friend. Understanding the market trends, property values, and neighborhood dynamics can significantly influence your investment decisions. Spend time exploring local listings, attending open houses, and talking to real estate agents. Knowledge is power, and the more you know, the better equipped you will be to make informed choices. This is where teamwork comes into play; share your findings with your friends, and brainstorm together about potential properties that align with your goals. Remember, every great empire starts with a solid foundation, and that foundation is built on research.

Next, consider the various financing options available to you. Traditional mortgages might seem out of reach, but creative financing methods open up many doors. Look into cooperative investment strategies where you and your friends pool your resources to buy a property together. By leveraging each other's strengths, you can minimize risk and maximize potential returns. This collaborative approach not only makes investing more accessible but also fosters teamwork and strengthens your friendship as you navigate the ups and downs of the real estate market.

Once you've secured a property, effective management becomes crucial. Low-cost property management techniques can keep your expenses down and profits high. For example, you can handle minor repairs yourselves or use online platforms for marketing your rental. House hacking is another smart strategy; consider renting out a room or a part of the property to generate income. This not only helps cover your mortgage but also teaches valuable lessons about managing tenants and maintaining a property. By working together, you can implement these strategies, learning and growing as you build your empire.

Lastly, building a real estate network is vital for long-term success. Attend local real estate meetups, join online forums, and connect with other young investors. Surrounding yourself with like-minded individuals can inspire new ideas and provide valuable insights into the market. Networking also opens up opportunities for joint ventures and partnerships, which can accelerate your growth and expand your reach. With determination, teamwork, and a commitment to learning, you and your friends can transform your twenty bucks a day into a thriving real estate empire, proving that age is just a number when it comes to chasing dreams.

Chapter 8

Budgeting for Success

The Importance of a Budget

A budget is like a roadmap for your financial journey, especially when it comes to building a real estate empire with your friends. Imagine embarking on an adventure without a clear direction; you might end up lost or going in circles. A budget helps you set your goals, allocate your resources wisely, and track your progress, ensuring that every dollar spent brings you closer to your dreams. For teenagers with limited funds, understanding the importance of budgeting can be the difference between merely dreaming about real estate success and actually achieving it.

Creating a budget allows you and your friends to see the bigger picture of your investment journey. It's not just about the $20 a day you have to spend; it's about how you use that money to leverage opportunities. By laying out your income and expenses, you can identify areas where you can save or invest more effectively. This clarity will empower you to make informed decisions, whether it's pooling your resources to buy a low-cost property or setting aside funds for unexpected repairs. Remember, every investment counts, and knowing where your money goes is the first step in making it work for you.

Budgeting also encourages teamwork and accountability among friends. When you collectively commit to a financial plan, you're not just looking out for yourself; you're supporting one another in achieving a shared goal. Regularly discussing your budget can foster open communication about your dreams, fears, and financial strategies. This collaboration strengthens your bond and helps you learn from one another's mistakes and successes. It's a powerful reminder that together, you can turn limited resources into a thriving real estate venture, proving that friendship can be a formidable asset in business.

Moreover, a well-structured budget opens the door to creative financing methods. With a clear understanding of your financial situation, you can explore innovative ways to fund your real estate ambitions. Whether it's house hacking, where you live in part of a property while renting out the rest, or finding cooperative investment strategies that allow you to pool resources with other investors, a budget provides the foundation for these creative solutions. You'll discover that there are many paths to financial success, and a budget can help you navigate them with ease and confidence.

Finally, mastering the art of budgeting equips you with invaluable skills that extend beyond real estate. The discipline you develop while managing your finances will serve you well in any future endeavor. It teaches you to think critically, plan ahead, and make strategic choices that align with your goals. As you and your friends embark on this journey to build your real estate empire, remember that a solid budget is not just a tool; it is a catalyst for your dreams. Embrace it, learn from it, and watch as it transforms your visions into reality.

Tracking Expenses and Income

Tracking your expenses and income is one of the most critical skills you can master as you embark on your real estate journey. For three friends dreaming big with just twenty bucks a day, keeping a close eye on every dollar spent and earned can be the difference between success and failure. This process not only helps you understand where your money goes but also empowers you to make informed decisions. By tracking your finances diligently, you lay the groundwork for a solid foundation in real estate investing.

Start by setting up a simple budgeting system. You don't need fancy software or complicated spreadsheets; a notepad or a basic app on your phone can do the trick. Create categories for your income and expenses—like property investments, repairs, utilities, and marketing. As you and your friends chip in your twenty bucks daily, keep a record of how much each person contributes and how that money is allocated. This practice fosters accountability and encourages everyone to stay engaged in the group's financial health.

Once you have a system in place, make it a habit to review your expenses and income regularly. Weekly or monthly check-ins can help you spot trends, identify areas where you can cut costs, and celebrate your financial victories, no matter how small. Tracking your progress together not only strengthens your bond as friends but also keeps everyone motivated. Remember, every dollar saved is a step closer to your real estate empire, and recognizing those small wins can fuel your drive to keep going.

As you start to see your real estate investments grow, consider the idea of reinvesting your profits. Discuss with your friends how you can use the income generated from your first property to fund the next one. This cooperative strategy can help you expand your portfolio without needing to dig into your personal savings. By keeping a meticulous record of your income, you will have clear insights into how much you can afford to reinvest, ensuring that you are making sound financial decisions for your group.

Finally, don't underestimate the power of networking and learning from others. Share your tracking methods and budgeting strategies with fellow young investors you meet along the way. Whether it's in a local meet-up or an online forum, these connections can provide you with new ideas and perspectives on how to manage your finances effectively in real estate. Building a network on a budget is not just about finding partners; it's about gaining knowledge and inspiration that can elevate your investment journey. By tracking your expenses and income diligently, you not only empower yourself but also inspire those around you to dream bigger and aim higher.

Saving Up for Your First Investment

Saving up for your first investment is an exciting journey that requires determination, creativity, and teamwork. As teenagers, you have the unique advantage of time on your side, allowing you to cultivate habits that will set the foundation for your financial future. Imagine pooling your resources with friends to create a small but mighty investment fund. With just twenty dollars a day, you can turn that modest amount into significant savings over time. Every dollar you save brings you one step closer to making your first real estate investment and building your dreams together.

Start by setting specific savings goals. Determine how much money you want to accumulate and by when you want to achieve that goal. For instance, if you aim to save up for a down payment on a property, break down the total amount into manageable milestones. This approach not only makes the goal feel achievable but also allows you to celebrate small victories along the way. By tracking your progress, you and your friends will remain motivated and accountable to each other, turning saving into a fun and engaging group activity.

Next, consider creative ways to save and earn money. This could include taking on part-time jobs or gig work that fits into your schedules, such as babysitting, tutoring, or even starting a small online business. Each of you can contribute your earnings to the investment fund, demonstrating the power of cooperative strategies among friends. Additionally, you can brainstorm ideas for cutting back on expenses, such as preparing meals together instead of eating out or sharing subscriptions to entertainment services. Every dollar saved is a dollar closer to your dream.

Don't underestimate the power of networking in your community. Start building connections with local real estate investors, attending workshops, and joining online forums related to real estate investing. These connections can provide valuable insights, tips, and potential investment opportunities that may not be available to the average person. As you learn more about the industry and start to build relationships, you may even find mentors who can guide you on your journey and help you navigate the complexities of real estate investing.

Lastly, remember that the journey of saving for your first investment is just as important as the investment itself. It's a time to learn about financial responsibility, collaboration, and the art of patience. As you and your friends work together to reach your goal, you'll develop skills that extend far beyond real estate. Embrace this experience, keep your dreams alive, and know that with teamwork and perseverance, you can turn your twenty bucks a day into a thriving real estate empire. The future is bright, and your dream is just around the corner.

Chapter 9

The Fundamentals of Real Estate Investing

The Foundation

In the journey of building a real estate empire, the foundation is not just about bricks and mortar; it's about the mindset and strategies that will propel you toward your dreams. Imagine three friends, united by a common goal, pooling together just twenty dollars a day. This simple act of collaboration becomes the seed for their future successes. Starting with a modest budget doesn't mean you can't achieve great things. Instead, it challenges you to think creatively, to explore innovative ways to invest, and to forge strong alliances that will support your ambitions.

The first step in laying your foundation is understanding the power of cooperative investment. When you team up with friends, you combine not just your financial resources, but also your unique skills and perspectives. One friend might be tech-savvy, another might have a knack for negotiation, while the third could be a whiz at marketing. By leveraging each other's strengths, you can tackle challenges more effectively and seize opportunities that would be daunting alone. This spirit of teamwork fosters an environment where everyone can learn and grow, turning what seems like a small sum into a launching pad for larger investments.

Creative financing methods also play a crucial role in building your foundation. When you're working with limited funds, traditional routes may not be feasible. However, there are numerous alternative strategies you can employ. For instance, consider seller financing, where the property owner allows you to pay in installments, or look into partnerships where you can share the investment risks and rewards. By thinking outside the box, you can unlock doors that might otherwise remain closed, allowing you to acquire properties without needing significant upfront capital.

As you embark on this adventure, mastering low-cost property management techniques is essential. Efficient management can dramatically increase your profitability, and there are plenty of ways to keep costs down. Embrace technology to streamline operations; simple apps can help you track expenses, communicate with tenants, and manage your properties more effectively. Additionally, learning basic maintenance skills can save you money and give you a sense of ownership over your investments. By keeping a tight rein on your expenses, you ensure that every dollar you earn gets reinvested back into your growing empire.

Lastly, building a real estate network on a budget is a vital part of your foundation. Your network is your net worth, and connecting with others in the industry opens up a world of opportunities. Attend local real estate meetings, join online forums, and engage with mentors who can share invaluable insights. These relationships can lead to partnerships, investment opportunities, and guidance that will help you navigate the complexities of real estate. Remember, every great empire was built by individuals who were not afraid to seek help and learn from others. As you strengthen your foundation, you're not just building a business; you're cultivating a community that will support your dreams for years to come.

Chapter 10

The $20 a Day Pact

The three friends' decision to save daily

In the heart of their small town, three friends sat around a table, each with a unique dream that brought them together: to build a real estate empire. Their aspirations were as grand as skyscrapers, but their pockets were far from deep. With just twenty bucks a day, they decided to embark on a journey that would require not only determination but also smart savings. They understood that every dollar spent recklessly was a step away from their dreams, so they made a pact to save diligently. This decision was the first steppingstone in their quest to transform their lives through real estate.

Each friend brought a different perspective to the table, enriching their approach to saving. One was a whiz at budgeting, always calculating how to stretch every dollar. Another had an eye for deals, believing that even a small amount could lead to big opportunities if invested wisely. The third was a natural leader, inspiring his friends to stay committed to their goal. They met regularly to discuss their progress, share tips, and motivate each other. This collective decision to save daily not only strengthened their friendship but also built a foundation of trust and accountability that was crucial for their future investments.

As their savings grew, the trio began to explore various avenues of real estate investing. They researched cooperative investment strategies that allowed them to pool their resources, making their dreams more attainable. They discovered that investing together not only minimized individual risk but also multiplied their potential rewards. With each dollar saved, they could tackle bigger projects, whether it was a rental property or a house that needed a little love. Their teamwork transformed their modest savings into a powerful tool for change.

Creativity became their best ally as they learned about financing methods that fit their budget. They explored low-cost property management techniques, ensuring that every penny they saved could be reinvested into their growing empire. They began to understand that real estate was not just about buying properties but also about managing them smartly. Each lesson they learned was a victory, and each victory brought them closer to their ultimate goal. Their daily savings of twenty bucks was no longer just about money; it became a symbol of their determination and commitment to success.

The friends realized that building a real estate network on a budget was just as important as saving money. They attended local meetups, volunteered at real estate events, and connected with mentors who shared their passion. With each new connection, they gained insight and resources that would help them in their journey. Their decision to save daily not only transformed their finances but also opened doors to opportunities they had never imagined. Together, they were not just saving money; they were building a future filled with possibility, one twenty-dollar bill at a time.

Initial $7,000 savings each and how they acquired their first $200,000 property

In the journey of building a real estate empire, it all starts with the right mindset and a little bit of savings. For our trio of friends, the goal was clear: to turn their collective dream into a reality. Each of them set aside $7,000, a sum that might seem modest in the grand scheme of real estate investing, but it represented a solid foundation. This initial $21,000 wasn't just money; it symbolized their commitment, teamwork, and belief in a brighter future together. With determination and creative thinking, they were ready to embark on their adventure.

Acquiring their first property required more than just their savings; it demanded strategic planning and innovative ideas. The friends spent countless hours researching properties in their local area, seeking opportunities that others might overlook. They leveraged online tools, attended local real estate meetups, and connected with seasoned investors. They learned about the art of negotiation and how to spot a good deal, realizing that every property has unique potential waiting to be unlocked. Their passion for learning and collaboration turned what seemed like a challenging task into an exhilarating quest.

After weeks of searching and analyzing, they stumbled upon a modest duplex that seemed perfect for their first investment. Priced at $200,000, it was slightly above their combined savings, but they saw the opportunity to turn it into a smart investment. Harnessing creative financing methods, they approached the seller with a win-win proposal, offering a combination of their savings as a down payment and a seller-financed option for the remaining balance. This strategy not only allowed them to secure the property but also showcased the power of teamwork and negotiation.

With the duplex under their control, the friends quickly realized the importance of effective property management. They divided responsibilities, with each friend taking charge of different aspects of managing the property. By utilizing low-cost property management techniques, they learned to handle maintenance issues themselves, market the rental units online, and even set up a budget to track expenses. Their cooperative investment strategy not only minimized costs but also strengthened their bond as friends and business partners.

As they settled into their new roles as real estate owners, the friends began to see the fruits of their labor. The rental income from the duplex not only covered their mortgage but also provided a steady cash flow. This success fueled their ambition, inspiring them to dream bigger and plan for future investments. By starting with just $7,000 each and leveraging their creativity, determination, and friendship, they transformed their initial investment into a launching pad for a thriving real estate empire. Their story serves as a reminder that with a shared vision and collaborative effort, anything is possible.

Chapter 11

Simple Math, Massive Dreams

How $20/day adds up over time

Imagine waking up one day and realizing that you have the power to turn a small daily habit into a life-changing investment strategy. Saving just $20 a day might seem insignificant at first, but when you start to visualize how that money can grow over time, a world of possibilities opens up. Each day, as you put aside that twenty-dollar bill, you are not just saving; you are building the foundation for your future. This simple act can set the stage for an incredible journey into real estate investing with your friends.

Let's break it down: saving $20 a day adds up to $140 a week, $600 a month, and an impressive $7,300 a year. Imagine pooling that money with your two best friends. Suddenly, you're looking at a staggering $21,900 after just three years! That's a solid chunk of change that can be put towards your first investment property. With the right mindset and commitment, you can transform that daily sacrifice into a steppingstone toward financial independence and wealth creation.

But it's not just about the numbers; it's also about the lessons learned along the way. By consistently saving and investing, you develop essential skills like discipline, budgeting, and teamwork. Working together with your friends on this journey fosters collaboration and trust, essential qualities when venturing into real estate. You'll learn to make collective decisions, evaluate properties, and explore financing options that cater to your group. This experience will not only strengthen your friendship but also prepare you for the challenges of the real estate market.

As you embark on this journey, consider the power of compound interest. By re-investing your savings into real estate, your money will work for you, growing exponentially over time. Think about how the value of properties can increase, how rental income can provide cash flow, and how each investment can lead to more opportunities. This is where creativity comes into play. You can explore house hacking, where you live in one part of a property while renting out the others, maximizing your investment and minimizing costs. Your initial $20 a day can morph into a sustainable income stream, propelling you and your friends into a thriving real estate empire.

Ultimately, the journey of saving $20 a day is about more than just the money. It's about dreaming big, setting goals, and taking action. As teenagers, you have the unique advantage of time on your side. The earlier you start saving and investing, the greater the rewards will be. By committing to this daily habit, you and your friends can pave the way for a future filled with opportunities, financial freedom, and the chance to create a lasting legacy in the world of real estate. So grab your friends, start saving, and watch how those twenty dollars a day turn into your dream come true.

Overview of 8% down payment strategy

In the journey of building a real estate empire, every dollar counts, and the 8% down payment strategy is a powerful tool that can help you and your friends make significant strides towards your dreams. Imagine pooling together your resources to invest in a property with just a small amount of money upfront. By contributing 8% of the purchase price, you can open the door to opportunities that may have seemed out of reach. This strategy allows you to leverage your collective funds effectively while minimizing the financial burden on each individual.

Using the 8% down payment approach means you can enter the real estate market sooner. Instead of waiting years to save for a traditional 20% down payment, which can feel daunting, you can jump in with a smaller amount. This can be especially motivating for teenagers who may have limited savings but plenty of ambition. The sooner you invest, the sooner you can start experiencing the benefits of property ownership, like rental income and potential appreciation in value.

The power of teamwork plays a crucial role in this strategy. By collaborating with friends, you can not only share the down payment but also divide the responsibilities of managing the property. This cooperative investment approach allows each member to contribute their unique skills, whether in property management, finding tenants, or handling finances. Working together not only makes the process easier but also fosters a sense of camaraderie and shared purpose, strengthening your friendships as you build your empire.

Creative financing methods can also complement the 8% down payment strategy, allowing you to maximize your investment potential. For example, consider finding properties that may need some work, which can often be purchased at a lower price. With your combined efforts, you can renovate these properties and increase their value while keeping your initial investment low. This not only gives you a chance to hone your skills in budgeting and project management but also teaches valuable lessons about real estate and teamwork.

As you embark on this journey, remember that building a real estate network is essential. Surround yourself with like-minded individuals who share your vision and can provide guidance or resources. Attend local workshops, join online forums, and connect with mentors who can help you navigate the complexities of real estate investing. The 8% down payment strategy is just one piece of the puzzle, but with determination, collaboration, and a supportive network, you and your friends can turn your twenty bucks a day into a thriving real estate empire.

Power of consistency, budgeting, and vision

In the journey of building a real estate empire, the power of consistency, budgeting, and vision cannot be overstated. Imagine three friends pooling together just twenty dollars a day. It may seem like a small amount, but with unwavering commitment and a clear vision, they can turn that modest sum into something incredible. Consistency is the secret ingredient that transforms dreams into reality. By setting aside time each day to learn about real estate, analyze properties, or network with others, they lay the foundation for success. It's not about how much money they start with; it's about how dedicated they are to their goals.

Budgeting is the backbone of any successful venture, especially when starting with limited resources. The friends must learn the art of managing their finances wisely. This means tracking every dollar they spend and ensuring they are investing in opportunities that align with their vision. By creating a budget, they can allocate funds not just for purchasing properties but also for education, networking, and unforeseen expenses. This careful planning empowers them to make informed decisions, allowing their twenty dollars a day to stretch further than they ever imagined.

A clear vision acts as a guiding star for these friends. It's not just about buying properties; it's about creating a legacy and building a future. They must define what success looks like for them. Is it financial freedom, the ability to travel, or providing homes for others? Whatever it may be, having a shared vision fosters unity and motivation. When challenges arise, which they inevitably will, this vision will remind them of their purpose and keep them focused on their ultimate goal. It's this clarity that drives them to work harder, stay consistent, and continue budgeting wisely.

Creative financing methods will play a crucial role in their journey. With limited funds, they need to think outside the box. This might mean exploring partnerships, seeking out sellers willing to finance a property, or even leveraging their skills to add value to a property before selling it for a profit. By embracing innovative strategies, they can turn obstacles into opportunities. The friends will learn that real estate isn't just about having money; it's about being resourceful and willing to take calculated risks.

Ultimately, building a real estate empire with just twenty dollars a day isn't just a dream; it's a realistic goal. When these friends commit to consistency, practice sound budgeting, and remain anchored to their vision, they can achieve extraordinary things. The journey might be challenging, but with determination and the right strategies, they will discover that they have what it takes to succeed. Each step they take together not only brings them closer to their dreams but also strengthens their bond as friends, proving that teamwork and shared aspirations can lead to remarkable achievements

Chapter 12

Principles of Collective Wealth

Why they chose to invest together

In the heart of every ambitious teenager lies a desire to dream big and make those dreams a reality. For three friends, the journey began with just twenty bucks a day. They chose to invest together not just to pool their resources, but to unite their unique strengths and visions. Each friend brought something different to the table—one had a keen eye for potential properties, another was a whiz with numbers, and the third had an innate ability to connect with people. This combination of skills created a solid foundation for their real estate empire, proving that when you work together, you can achieve more than you ever could alone.

The decision to invest as a group also came from a shared understanding of the challenges that young investors face. With limited funds and experience, navigating the real estate market can be daunting. By collaborating, they could tackle those challenges head-on. They learned together, shared responsibilities, and supported each other through the highs and lows of property investing. This cooperative strategy not only minimized individual risk but also maximized their chances of success. Teenage dreams became actionable plans as they discovered that teamwork could transform their modest investment into something monumental.

Moreover, investing together allowed them to access opportunities that might have been out of reach if they had gone solo. By combining their twenty-dollar-a-day contributions, they could save faster for down payments and invest in properties that offered greater potential for returns. They quickly realized that even small amounts could lead to significant results over time, especially when leveraged creatively. This approach to budgeting and investing ignited their imaginations and expanded their horizons, illustrating that financial success is not just for the wealthy, but achievable for anyone willing to work together and think outside the box.

As they navigated the world of real estate, the friends also discovered the importance of building a network. They attended workshops, connected with mentors, and engaged with other young investors. Each interaction brought new ideas and strategies, sharpening their skills and expanding their understanding of the industry. Their collective enthusiasm attracted others who were eager to join their journey. This growing community became a valuable resource, reinforcing the idea that collaboration is key to success in real estate. Through networking, they learned not just about properties, but about the power of shared knowledge and support.

Ultimately, their journey was not just about making money; it was about friendship and growth. By choosing to invest together, they cultivated a sense of camaraderie that transcended financial goals. They celebrated each small victory and learned from their mistakes, all while fostering a deep bond that would last a lifetime. Their story serves as an inspiration for other teenagers: the dream of building a real estate empire is within reach, especially when approached with creativity, collaboration, and a shared sense of purpose.

Legal structures, trust, and responsibility

When embarking on a journey to build a real estate empire with your friends, understanding legal structures, trust, and responsibility is crucial. Imagine your group as a team of superheroes, each with unique abilities and roles. To succeed, you need to establish a solid foundation that not only protects your interests but also fosters collaboration and trust among you. This foundation often takes the form of legal agreements or partnerships, which can be as simple as a handshake or as complex as formal contracts, depending on the scale of your investment.

Choosing the right legal structure is like selecting the best tools for your adventure. You might opt for a partnership, where each friend's contribution and role are clearly defined, allowing for shared profits and responsibilities. Alternatively, a limited liability company (LLC) can provide a safety net, protecting your personal assets from any potential pitfalls in your real estate endeavors. Understanding these options is essential, as they help you navigate the responsibilities that come with ownership and investment, ensuring that everyone is on the same page and committed to the journey.

Trust is the glue that binds your group together. Just like a tree grows stronger with deep roots, your investment group thrives on mutual respect and reliability. Open communication is key—discuss your goals, expectations, and any fears openly. When everyone feels heard and valued, it creates a supportive environment where each person can contribute their ideas and energy. Trust also means holding each other accountable; if one friend falls short on their responsibilities, it can affect the whole group. Establishing clear roles and expectations from the start can help mitigate misunderstandings and strengthen your bond.

Taking on responsibility is not only about managing properties but also about being a dependable partner. As you dive into property management, remember that each decision you make impacts your friends and your shared goals. Whether it's dealing with tenants, handling finances, or renovating a property, having a responsible approach ensures that everyone's investment is safeguarded. Embrace the challenges as learning opportunities; every obstacle overcome together will enhance your teamwork and deepen the trust you've built.

In the end, the journey to building a real estate empire is about more than just financial success; it's about growing together as friends and partners. By establishing strong legal structures, fostering trust, and embracing responsibility, you create a supportive environment that encourages creativity and innovation. As you navigate this exciting path, remember that the friendships you build and the lessons you learn will be just as valuable as the properties you acquire. With determination and teamwork, your dream of owning real estate can become a reality, one day at a time.

Biblical and practical wisdom on partnership

Partnership in real estate, much like friendship, is strengthened through trust, communication, and shared vision. In the Bible, Ecclesiastes 4:9-10 teaches us that "two are better than one, because they have a good reward for their labor." This principle is pivotal for young investors. When you and your friends come together, pooling your resources and skills, you increase your chances of success. Just as Jesus surrounded himself with a diverse group of followers, your partnership can thrive when each member brings unique strengths to the table. Embracing this collaborative spirit can elevate your real estate journey from mere investment to a shared adventure.

Practical wisdom suggests that before diving into a partnership, you should establish clear goals. Discuss what success looks like for each of you and create a shared vision. This prevents misunderstandings and ensures everyone is on the same page. Proverbs 15:22 tells us, "Without counsel plans fail, but with many advisers, they succeed." By consulting with one another and making collective decisions, you can navigate the challenges of real estate investing together. Remember, it's essential to maintain open lines of communication, ensuring no one feels left out or overwhelmed.

Another vital aspect of partnership is accountability. Just as in the story of the Good Samaritan, where compassion and support are key, your partnership should be rooted in mutual respect and responsibility. Set up regular check-ins to discuss progress, challenges, and future plans. This not only keeps everyone accountable but also fosters a supportive environment where each member feels valued. By sharing both successes and setbacks, you can learn from each experience and grow stronger as a team.

Incorporating creative financing methods can also enhance your partnership's potential. As young investors, exploring options like house hacking or cooperative investment strategies can turn your dreams into reality without overwhelming financial burdens. The Bible encourages innovation and wisdom, as seen in Proverbs 8:12, which states, "I, wisdom, dwell with prudence, and I find knowledge and discretion." By leveraging each other's resources and knowledge, you can find unique opportunities that fit your budget while maximizing returns. Together, you can brainstorm ideas that may not be possible alone.

Lastly, building a real estate network is essential for long-term success. Just as the early Christians formed communities to support one another, your group can connect with other investors and mentors. Attend local real estate meetups, workshops, or online forums to expand your knowledge and resources. Surrounding yourselves with like-minded individuals can inspire new ideas and strategies, while also providing valuable insights into the market. Remember, partnership extends beyond just your immediate circle; it's about creating a community that uplifts and empowers each other on the path to building your real estate empire.

Chapter 13

One House a Year — The Plan in Motion

Step-by-step on acquiring one property each year

Acquiring one property each year may seem like a daunting task, especially when starting with just twenty bucks a day. However, with determination, teamwork, and a solid plan, you and your friends can transform that initial investment into a thriving real estate empire. The key is to break down the process into manageable steps that will guide you through the journey. By working together and leveraging your resources, you can achieve your goals and create wealth for your future.

First, begin by setting a clear vision of what you want to achieve. Discuss your dreams and goals with your friends, ensuring everyone is on the same page. Identify the type of properties you want to invest in, whether it be single-family homes, multi-family units, or even commercial spaces. Research your local market to determine which areas show potential for growth, affordability, and appeal. Establish a timeline for acquiring your first property and make a commitment to stick to it. This shared vision will serve as your foundation, motivating you through the ups and downs of the investment journey.

Next, it's time to strategize your finances. With only twenty dollars a day, you'll need to be creative in saving and pooling your resources. Encourage each friend to contribute a portion of their earnings, and explore ways to cut unnecessary expenses. Consider taking on side gigs or part-time jobs to increase your investment fund. In addition, familiarize yourselves with creative financing methods such as seller financing, partnerships, or even crowdfunding. By thinking outside the box, you can unlock opportunities that may not be available through traditional means.

Once your financial strategy is in place, the next step is to educate yourselves on the property acquisition process. Attend workshops or online courses, read books, and engage with real estate forums to learn about the ins and outs of buying properties. Networking is crucial at this stage; connect with local real estate agents, investors, and mentors who can provide valuable insights. Build a support system that will help you navigate challenges and celebrate your successes. Remember, knowledge is power, and the more informed you are, the better equipped you'll be to make smart investment decisions.

Finally, take action and make your first purchase! Start by scouting properties within your budget and conducting thorough due diligence on each option. Once you find a potential investment, work together to analyze its profitability, taking into account renovation costs, rental income, and potential appreciation. When you're ready to make an offer, ensure that you have a solid plan for property management. Whether you choose to manage the property yourselves or hire a property manager, having a clear strategy will help streamline operations and maximize your returns. As you close the deal, celebrate this milestone together, knowing that you have taken a significant step toward building your real estate empire. Each year, as you repeat this process, you will gain experience, confidence, and a growing portfolio that reflects the power of teamwork and perseverance.

Rental income, mortgage, and reinvestment approach

In the journey of building a real estate empire, understanding the relationship between rental income, mortgage payments, and reinvestment is key. Imagine pooling together twenty bucks a day with your friends to not just dream, but to actually create a path toward financial freedom. Each dollar you set aside can become a stepping stone towards owning properties that generate income. As you start to accumulate savings, think about how this money can be used strategically to invest in properties that will bring in rental income. This income becomes the fuel for your real estate ambitions.

When you purchase a property, you'll likely need to secure a mortgage. This is where your teamwork and collective knowledge come into play. By sharing responsibilities and researching mortgage options together, you can find the best deals that allow you to minimize costs. Remember, the goal is to leverage your investments wisely. A mortgage can seem intimidating at first, but with a solid understanding of how it works, you and your friends can navigate this process confidently. Each mortgage payment you make is an investment in your future, building equity in the property that can be used for further investments.

As you receive rental income from your properties, it's vital to have a clear plan for reinvestment. Rather than splurging on unnecessary expenses, consider reinvesting a significant portion of that income back into your real estate ventures. This could mean saving for a down payment on your next property or perhaps upgrading your current rental to attract higher-paying tenants. By focusing on reinvestment, you're not just growing your portfolio; you're also creating a sustainable cycle of wealth that benefits all of you as a team.

Creative financing methods can also play a significant role in maximizing your rental income and minimizing your mortgage burdens. Think outside the box—could you negotiate lower interest rates, or explore alternative funding options like partnerships or crowdfunding? The more you learn about these strategies, the more empowered you'll feel to take bold steps in your investment journey. Remember, every challenge you face is an opportunity to learn and innovate, and working together makes tackling these challenges much easier.

Finally, don't underestimate the power of building a network. Connecting with other young investors, real estate professionals, and mentors can open doors to opportunities you'd never imagine. Attend local meetups, join online forums, and engage with others who share your passion. Building a strong network will provide you with valuable insights, tips, and potential partnerships that can accelerate your growth. Together, with your friends by your side, you can turn that twenty bucks a day into a flourishing real estate empire. Keep dreaming big, stay focused, and let your journey inspire others along the way.

Chapter 14

The Equity Explosion Begins

Year 6: First equity withdrawal of $21,000

In the sixth year of our journey, we reached a significant milestone: our first equity withdrawal of $21,000. This moment wasn't just about the money; it was a testament to the power of teamwork, creativity, and our shared vision. We had started with just twenty bucks a day, and now, those small sacrifices had transformed into tangible success. This experience taught us that patience, persistence, and a strong bond among friends can lead to incredible achievements in real estate.

As teenagers, we often feel pressured to follow the conventional paths laid out for us. However, our journey demonstrated that we could carve our own routes. We had learned the ins and outs of budget real estate investing, and each step we took—every dollar saved and every hour spent researching—was a building block for our future. The equity withdrawal wasn't just a financial decision; it symbolized our ability to leverage our hard work and the lessons we had learned along the way.

The decision to withdraw equity was strategic. We evaluated our properties, assessed their current value, and realized that we had built enough equity to make a significant move. This was also a moment of affirmation for us; we were no longer just kids dreaming about real estate. We were young investors taking calculated risks and making money work for us. It was an empowering realization that we could control our financial future through informed decisions and cooperative investment strategies.

With the $21,000 in hand, we had the opportunity to reinvest and expand our empire. We brainstormed ways to use the funds effectively, considering creative financing methods that would allow us to acquire more properties without breaking the bank. Each idea sparked excitement and fuelled our ambition. We understood that this was just the beginning; with every investment, we were building a network of opportunities that would pave the way for even greater success.

As we reflected on our journey, we realized that this equity withdrawal wasn't just about numbers; it was about the friendships forged, the lessons learned, and the dreams we were manifesting together. We had embraced house hacking and low-cost property management techniques, and we were now ready to take on the next chapter of our adventure as a cohesive unit. United by a common goal, we were ready to tackle challenges and seize opportunities, proving to ourselves and others that with determination and teamwork, anything is possible.

Buying two houses instead of one

Buying two houses instead of one might sound a bit ambitious, especially when you're just starting with a limited budget. However, when you think creatively and act as a team, this strategy can transform your real estate journey from a dream into a thriving reality. Imagine pooling your resources with your friends and investing in two properties that can not only generate income but also provide valuable experiences. By embracing this approach, you can learn the ins and outs of real estate while maximizing your potential for growth.

The first step in this journey is understanding the power of cooperative investment. When you and your friends come together, you can combine your financial strengths. Instead of each person saving for one house, think about how pooling your funds can allow you to secure two properties. This collaborative effort can lead to greater financial stability and reduce individual risk. By working together, you can tackle challenges, share responsibilities, and celebrate successes as a cohesive unit. This camaraderie not only makes the process more enjoyable but also instills a sense of accountability among friends.

House hacking is a fantastic strategy that fits perfectly into this two-house concept. Picture this: you buy a duplex or a property with an additional unit, and one of you lives in one part while renting out the other. This arrangement not only covers your mortgage but also provides you with valuable experience in property management. You can apply these lessons to the second property, turning it into another source of income. By living in one unit, you reduce your living expenses while simultaneously investing in your future. This smart strategy turns your home into an asset rather than a liability.

Creative financing methods open up even more possibilities for acquiring two properties. Instead of traditional financing, explore options like seller financing, partnerships, or even crowdfunding. These methods can help you secure a second property without needing a hefty down payment upfront. Consider seeking out motivated sellers who may be willing to negotiate terms that work for everyone involved. By thinking outside the box, you can uncover opportunities that others might overlook. This is where your entrepreneurial spirit shines, turning a limited budget into a powerful investment strategy.

Lastly, building a real estate network is crucial as you embark on this journey. Attend local real estate meetups, join online forums, and connect with others who share your passion for investing. By establishing relationships with experienced investors, you can gain insights and tips that can help you navigate the complexities of buying two houses. These connections can lead to partnerships, mentorships, and even potential investment opportunities. Remember, every successful real estate empire starts with a single step, and with determination and teamwork, you and your friends can turn your twenty bucks a day into a thriving real estate portfolio.

Strategy for compounding properties annually

Compounding properties annually is a powerful strategy that can take your real estate dreams from a simple idea to a thriving empire. Imagine starting with just $20 a day, pooling your resources with friends, and watching your investments grow year after year. The magic of compounding lies in the way it allows your initial investment to generate returns, which then generate even more returns. By understanding and applying this concept, you can set the foundation for a successful real estate journey, even on a budget.

To begin your compounding journey, focus on acquiring your first property. This could be a small rental unit or even a house that you can house hack with your friends. The key is to find a property that not only fits your budget but also has the potential for appreciation. When you purchase a property, you're not just buying a physical space; you're investing in an asset that can grow in value over time. With a little creativity in financing and a solid plan for property management, you can turn that initial investment into a cash-producing asset that will serve you well for years to come.

Once you have your first property, it's crucial to reinvest the profits. Instead of spending the rental income on luxuries, consider putting that money back into the real estate market. This could mean saving for a down payment on a second property or using the funds for renovations to increase the value of your current property. Each dollar you reinvest is a step closer to multiplying your wealth. By making this a habit, you create a cycle of growth that can exponentially increase your holdings and financial security.

Building a real estate network is also essential for compounding your properties. Connect with other aspiring investors, local real estate professionals, and mentors who can provide guidance and opportunities. Attend workshops, join online forums, and engage in community groups focused on real estate. The more people you know, the more chances you have to find great deals and learn about effective strategies. This network can become a vital resource, offering insights that will help you make informed decisions and accelerate your investment journey.

Lastly, never underestimate the power of teamwork among friends. When you collaborate with your friends, you not only share the financial burden but also combine your strengths and skills. This cooperative approach can lead to innovative solutions and creative financing methods that can further enhance your investment strategy. Together, you can brainstorm ideas for managing properties more efficiently or coming up with unique ways to market your rentals. The camaraderie and shared vision can propel you forward, making the process not just a financial endeavor but a rewarding adventure that strengthens your friendships and builds a lasting real estate empire.

Chapter 15

A System that Builds Itself

Years 7 to 10: How withdrawals from equity fueled growth

If building a real estate empire, the years 7 to 10 were pivotal for the trio of friends, each taking bold steps fueled by their earlier successes. As they learned the ropes of real estate investment, they realized that their initial capital could be significantly boosted by strategic withdrawals from their growing equity. This was not just about financial gain; it was about believing in their dreams and the power of teamwork. Each decision became a stepping stone, proving that with a little creativity and collaboration, they could transform their $20-a-day habit into a robust real estate portfolio.

Equity became the engine of their growth. With every property they acquired, each friend contributed to the renovations and improvements, increasing the value of their investments. They understood that by leveraging the equity they built, they could reinvest in additional properties. This strategy allowed them to make calculated withdrawals, using the increased value of their existing properties to fund new purchases. It was a cycle of growth that fueled their ambitions and showcased how smart financial decisions could lead to extraordinary outcomes. They learned to see their equity not just as numbers on a balance sheet, but as a powerful tool for expansion.

The friends also explored creative financing methods, which transformed their approach to investing. They discovered that traditional banks were not the only option for funding. They ventured into partnerships and cooperative investment strategies, pooling resources and sharing risks. By collaborating with other like-minded individuals, they unlocked opportunities that would have otherwise been out of reach. This cooperative spirit was not just about monetary support; it was about building a network of trust and shared vision, reinforcing the idea that together, they could achieve far more than they could alone.

Low-cost property management techniques became their secret weapon. Rather than spending extensively on property management services, the trio decided to manage their properties themselves. They developed a hands-on approach, learning the ins and outs of maintenance, tenant relations, and marketing. This not only saved them money, but also deepened their understanding of the real estate market. They became more than investors; they became adept property managers, capable of navigating challenges and optimizing their investments for maximum return. Their commitment to learning and adapting was a testament to their dream of building something substantial.

As they moved through these formative years, the friends realized that their journey was not just about acquiring properties, but about fostering a mindset of growth and resilience. They inspired each other to think bigger and take risks. House hacking became a popular strategy among them, allowing them to live in one property while renting out the others. This not only helped cover their living expenses but also created a steady income stream. Their story became a beacon of hope for other teenagers looking to forge their own paths in real estate, proving that with dedication, creativity, and a solid network, dreams could indeed become reality.

Annual rituals: saving, buying, renting, refinancing

In the journey of building a real estate empire, annual rituals become the backbone of your financial strategy. For teenagers with dreams as grand as theirs, saving money is the first step. It's not just about putting away a few bucks here and there; it's about developing a mindset of growth and opportunity. Imagine setting aside a portion of your weekly allowance or earnings from a part-time job. By consistently saving, even small amounts, you create a cushion that will enable you to seize opportunities when they arise. Each dollar saved is a step closer to your dream, and together, with your friends, you can turn those savings into something monumental.

Buying property can seem daunting, especially on a tight budget. However, with a collective mindset, it transforms into an exciting adventure. Consider pooling your resources with friends to make a joint purchase. This strategy not only makes properties more accessible but also allows you to share responsibilities and benefits. By researching affordable neighborhoods and understanding market trends, you can identify investment opportunities that align with your collective vision. Every property acquired is not just a brick-and-mortar investment; it symbolizes your shared commitment and ambition to succeed together.

Renting is another vital ritual that can be turned into an advantage. Instead of viewing it as a mere expense, see it as a steppingstone to future investments. Renting a property as a group can lower individual costs while providing valuable living and management experience. Use this time to hone your property management skills, learn how to negotiate leases, and understand tenant needs. The lessons learned during this renting phase will be invaluable when you step into the role of property owners, equipping you with the knowledge to build a stronger real estate portfolio.

Refinancing is often overlooked by beginners, yet it can be a powerful tool in your investment strategy. As you grow and properties appreciate, consider the benefits of refinancing to lower your monthly payments or to pull out equity for new investments. This process allows you to leverage previous successes into future opportunities. By regularly reviewing your financial position, you and your friends can make informed decisions that enhance your investment potential. Refinancing isn't just about saving money; it's about strategically positioning yourselves to expand your empire.

Incorporating these annual rituals—saving, buying, renting, and refinancing—into your lives will not only set you on a path to financial success but will also strengthen the bonds of friendship. Each step you take together is a testament to your shared dreams and ambitions. Celebrate your achievements, learn from your challenges, and keep pushing forward. With determination and teamwork, the dream of building a real estate empire is not just a fantasy; it's an attainable reality. Embrace these rituals, and watch as your collective efforts transform twenty bucks a day into a thriving real estate legacy

Chapter 16

The Wealth Impact

The journey of building a real estate empire,

The journey of building a real estate empire, even on a limited budget, is not just about the money you make; it's also about the wealth you create in your life and the lives of those around you. For three friends starting with just twenty bucks a day, the possibilities are vast and exciting. By pooling their resources, they not only invest in properties but also invest in each other's dreams and aspirations. This cooperative spirit transforms their financial landscape, proving that wealth is not solely measured in dollars but also in the relationships and experiences that come along the way.

When you think about wealth, it's easy to focus on the tangible aspects—money, property, and assets. However, wealth also encompasses knowledge, skills, and connections. As these three friends embark on their real estate adventure, they learn about creative financing methods that allow them to stretch their budget further than they ever thought possible. They discover innovative ways to negotiate deals, leverage partnerships, and find hidden gems in the real estate market that others overlook. This knowledge becomes an invaluable asset, empowering them to make informed decisions and take calculated risks.

Living on twenty bucks a day may seem limiting at first, but this challenge forces the friends to think outside the box. They explore low-cost property management techniques that help them maintain their investments without breaking the bank. From DIY repairs to using technology for efficient communication with tenants, they find ways to keep their expenses low while maximizing their returns. This resourcefulness not only strengthens their financial position but also builds their confidence as young entrepreneurs. They learn that the ability to adapt and innovate is a powerful form of wealth in itself.

Building a real estate network on a budget is another critical aspect of their journey. The friends realize that connecting with others in the industry can open doors they never imagined. They attend local meetups, join online forums, and reach out to mentors who share their expertise. These relationships provide valuable insights and opportunities that help the trio grow their investments even further. By fostering a supportive community around them, they not only enhance their own prospects but also contribute to the success of their peers. Together, they create a ripple effect that benefits everyone involved.

Ultimately, the wealth impact of their journey is profound. As they navigate the ups and downs of real estate investing, they cultivate a mindset of abundance and possibility. They understand that true wealth is about more than financial gains; it's about the joy of achieving goals together, the thrill of learning, and the satisfaction of helping others along the way. By sharing their experiences, they inspire other teenagers to dream big, think creatively, and embark on their own paths to financial freedom. Through determination, collaboration, and a commitment to each other, these three friends prove that even the smallest beginnings can lead to extraordinary outcomes.

Chapter 17
Year 10 Milestone

Number of homes owned

In the journey of building a real estate empire with just twenty bucks a day, understanding the number of homes owned is a crucial milestone. For teenagers dreaming of financial independence, the idea of owning properties might seem daunting, but it can also be incredibly exciting. Each home represents not just a piece of real estate but a step towards achieving your dreams. By pooling resources with friends, you can turn a seemingly impossible goal into a tangible reality. Imagine the thrill of celebrating your first property purchase together, knowing that you've taken the initial steps to create a legacy.

Every home you own can serve multiple purposes, making your investments more versatile. You can rent them out, live in them, or even turn them into vacation rentals. This flexibility offers incredible opportunities for teenagers like you to experiment and learn about the world of real estate. By starting small and focusing on the number of homes owned, you can gain valuable experience in property management, tenant relationships, and market analysis. Each property adds to your portfolio and builds your confidence in making informed investment decisions.

Cooperative investment strategies among friends can be particularly powerful when it comes to increasing the number of homes owned. By working together, you can share the costs and responsibilities associated with buying and maintaining properties. This teamwork not only spreads financial risk but also fosters a sense of camaraderie and joint purpose. Imagine sitting down with your friends, discussing potential properties, and making collective decisions that will shape your financial future. Every home you acquire is a testament to your collaborative spirit and shared vision.

Creative financing methods can also play a pivotal role in increasing the number of homes you own. Many young investors assume that they need a hefty sum of money to get started, but that's not the case. There are countless ways to secure financing without breaking the bank. From seller financing to lease options, these techniques allow you to acquire properties with minimal upfront costs. Learning about these methods can empower you to seize opportunities that others might overlook, ultimately leading to a robust portfolio of homes.

Finally, as you build your real estate network on a budget, the number of homes owned will become a reflection of your growing influence and expertise in the field. Networking with other investors, mentors, and real estate professionals can open doors to exclusive deals and insights that can propel your journey forward. Each connection you make can lead to new opportunities, partnerships, and resources that enhance your ability to acquire more properties. As you navigate this exciting path, remember that every home owned is not just an investment; it's a step towards your dream of financial freedom and a testament to the power of friendship and collaboration.

Annual rental cash flow

Annual rental cash flow is the lifeblood of any successful real estate venture, and understanding it is crucial for you and your friends as you embark on this exciting journey. Think of rental cash flow as the money you make from your properties after covering all your expenses. This money can propel your dreams forward, allowing you to reinvest, travel, or even throw an epic party to celebrate your achievements. By grasping how to calculate and maximize your annual rental cash flow, you'll be well on your way to building your own real estate empire.

To start, you'll want to learn how to calculate your annual rental cash flow. Begin by determining your total rental income. If you're renting out a property for $1,200 a month, that translates to $14,400 a year. Next, subtract your operating expenses, which include property management fees, maintenance, insurance, taxes, and any utilities you cover. For example, if your annual expenses total $6,000, your rental cash flow would be $8,400. This number is key to understanding how much profit you're generating and how you can use it to grow your portfolio.

Now that you know how to calculate your cash flow, the focus shifts to enhancing it. One of the most effective ways to boost your income is through house hacking. This involves renting out a portion of your home, such as a spare room or a basement apartment, to help cover your mortgage and expenses. Not only does this strategy create additional cash flow, but it also allows you to live in a property while others contribute to its costs. Imagine splitting the rent with your friends, turning your living space into a mini real estate venture and gaining valuable management experience along the way.

Creative financing methods can also increase your annual rental cash flow. Instead of relying solely on traditional bank loans, explore options like seller financing, where the property owner agrees to finance the sale directly. This can provide you with more favorable terms and lower initial costs, leaving more room in your budget for other investments. Additionally, consider partnering with your friends to pool your resources. This cooperative investment strategy not only reduces individual financial burdens but also enhances your collective purchasing power, enabling you to acquire properties that might otherwise be out of reach.

Lastly, as you build your real estate network on a budget, remember that connections can lead to new opportunities and improved cash flow. Attend local real estate meetups, join online forums, and engage with fellow investors who share your passion. By sharing strategies, tips, and resources, you can collectively enhance your understanding of rental cash flow and discover innovative ways to optimize your investments. Together, with the right knowledge and teamwork, you can turn that initial twenty bucks into a thriving real estate empire, creating a future full of possibilities.

Total equity and net worth

Total equity and net worth are two essential concepts in real estate investing that can seem complicated at first, but they are straightforward once you break them down. For young investors like you, understanding these terms is crucial as you embark on your journey with your friends to build a real estate empire on a budget. Total equity refers to the value of your property minus what you owe on it, while net worth is the sum of all your assets, including your properties, minus your liabilities. This means that every smart investment you make with your twenty bucks a day not only contributes to your equity but also to your overall net worth.

Imagine you and your friends manage to scrape together a down payment for a small rental property. The moment you close the deal, you start building equity. Each month, as you pay down the mortgage, your equity increases. This is your financial stake in the property, and it grows as the property appreciates over time. Every dollar you invest isn't just a cost; it's a step toward your financial freedom and long-term wealth. By strategically selecting properties in up-and-coming neighborhoods, you can maximize your equity growth, turning your initial investment into a thriving asset.

Net worth, on the other hand, gives you a broader picture of your financial health. As you build your real estate portfolio, keep track of all your assets, such as cash, savings, and the value of your properties, against your liabilities, like loans or credit card debt. This exercise helps you understand where you stand financially and what steps you need to take to elevate your situation. By treating your real estate investments not just as individual properties but as part of a larger financial strategy, you empower yourselves to make informed decisions that will benefit you in the long run.

Collaborative investment strategies are a fantastic way to enhance both equity and net worth among friends. Pooling your resources allows you to leverage each other's strengths and financial capabilities, making it easier to invest in larger properties or multiple units. With creativity and teamwork, you can explore low-cost property management techniques and house hacking strategies that will not only minimize expenses but also maximize profits. This collaborative approach creates a supportive environment where you can learn from one another, share risks, and celebrate successes together.

Ultimately, as you embark on this adventure of building a real estate empire, remember that every step you take today lays the foundation for your future. Focus on increasing your total equity and net worth, and keep your eyes on the bigger picture. The journey may have its challenges, but with determination, creativity, and the support of your friends, you can turn those twenty bucks a day into a wealth-building machine. Embrace the possibilities that lie ahead, and let your dreams of financial independence become a reality through smart real estate investments.

Chapter 18

Year 15 Growth

Expanded Portfolio

Expanded portfolio

In the journey of building a real estate empire, expanding your portfolio is not just a dream; it's a strategy that can propel you toward financial freedom. Imagine pooling your resources with friends, where each contribution, no matter how small, acts as a steppingstone to greater opportunities. With just $20 a day, you and your friends can explore various avenues in real estate that might once have seemed out of reach. The key is to think creatively and collaboratively, turning small investments into significant returns.

One exciting way to expand your portfolio is through cooperative investment strategies. By teaming up with your friends, you can combine your financial power to purchase properties that may otherwise be unattainable. Each member of the group can take charge of different aspects of the investment, from property management to marketing. This division of labor not only makes the process more manageable but also allows you to learn from one another, gaining invaluable experience in the real estate market. Together, you can tackle larger projects, such as multi-family homes or commercial spaces, that can generate multiple streams of income.

Creative financing methods can also play a vital role in expanding your portfolio without requiring a hefty upfront investment. There are numerous strategies you can employ, such as seller financing, lease options, or partnerships that minimize initial costs. These methods allow you to acquire properties with little money down, enabling you and your friends to leverage your limited resources effectively. As you learn to navigate these creative financing options, you'll discover that real estate doesn't have to be an exclusive club for those with deep pockets; it's a field ripe for innovation and teamwork.

House hacking is another powerful tool in your arsenal. This strategy involves purchasing a property and renting out part of it to cover your mortgage and expenses. With your friends, you can buy a larger property together, live in one part, and rent out the rest. This not only reduces your living costs but also allows you to build equity over time. Imagine sharing a house with your friends while simultaneously investing in your future. House hacking transforms living expenses into an investment opportunity, making it a win-win for everyone involved.

Lastly, building a real estate network on a budget is crucial for ongoing success in your investment journey. Connect with local real estate groups, attend workshops, and engage in online forums to meet like-minded individuals. Your friendship group can serve as a strong foundation, but expanding your network opens doors to mentorship, partnerships, and new investment opportunities. Surrounding yourself with experienced investors can provide insights and guidance that will help you navigate challenges and seize opportunities. Remember, every successful investor started with a dream, and together, you and your friends can transform your $20 a day into a flourishing real estate empire.

Increased rents and reduced mortgage balances

In the ever-evolving world of real estate, the dynamic relationship between increased rents and reduced mortgage balances presents an exciting opportunity for young investors like you. Imagine your dreams of financial independence and wealth-building coming to life, fueled by the simple yet powerful principle that as rents rise, your potential for profit grows. This concept isn't just a financial statistic; it's a chance for you and your friends to turn a modest daily investment into a thriving real estate empire.

As rents in your area begin to climb, the value of the properties you might invest in also increases. This is particularly beneficial for you as a budding investor. With every dollar you save and invest, you are not just contributing to your own future; you are participating in a market where your investments can appreciate over time. Your friends can pool their resources—just twenty bucks a day can go a long way when combined. This collective effort amplifies your purchasing power and opens doors to opportunities that might have seemed out of reach.

Moreover, as mortgage balances reduce over time, the financial burden on you and your friends lessens. This reduction means that your cash flow improves, allowing for more flexibility in your investments. You may find that the properties you manage or invest in start generating positive cash flow sooner than expected. This newfound financial freedom can be reinvested into more properties, further increasing your net worth and reinforcing the concept of 'house hacking,' where you can live in one unit while renting out others to cover your expenses.

Engaging in cooperative investment strategies among friends not only builds camaraderie but also enhances your collective knowledge and experience. You can learn from each other's successes and mistakes, creating a supportive network that encourages smart decision-making. With your daily contributions, you can explore creative financing methods that allow you to acquire properties with little money down, leveraging your combined skills to tackle challenges head-on. This approach transforms setbacks into stepping stones for success.

As you embark on this journey, remember that building a real estate network on a budget is essential. Attend local workshops, join online forums, and seek mentors who can guide you. Surrounding yourselves with like-minded individuals who share your dreams will inspire you to stay committed. Increased rents and reduced mortgage balances are not just figures; they are the stepping stones to your future. With determination, creativity, and teamwork, you and your friends can turn those twenty bucks a day into a flourishing real estate empire that will support your dreams for years to come.

Appreciation and tax benefits

Appreciation in real estate is one of the most exciting aspects of investing, especially for young dreamers like you who are starting with just twenty bucks a day. When you invest in properties, you're not just buying a piece of land or a structure; you're acquiring an asset that can grow in value over time. Think of it as planting a seed in a garden. With care, attention, and the right environment, that seed can blossom into a flourishing tree, providing shade and fruits for years to come. As your properties appreciate, the equity you build can be a powerful tool to reinvest and expand your real estate empire.

Understanding tax benefits is equally crucial for young investors. Taxes can feel overwhelming, but they also offer opportunities to keep more money in your pocket. For instance, property owners can often deduct mortgage interest, property taxes, and even certain expenses related to managing and maintaining the property. This means that every dollar you spend on improving your investment could potentially reduce your taxable income, allowing you to reinvest those savings into more properties. By familiarizing yourself with these benefits early on, you're setting yourself up for financial success.

Cooperative investment strategies among friends can amplify the benefits of appreciation and tax savings. When three friends pool their resources, they not only share the financial burden but also the potential rewards. Imagine if each of you contributes a small amount each day towards a shared real estate goal. Together, you can afford better properties, manage expenses more effectively, and take advantage of larger tax deductions. This collaborative approach can create a supportive environment where everyone learns from each other, leading to smarter investment decisions.

Creative financing methods can also play a significant role in your journey. Instead of relying solely on traditional loans, explore options like seller financing or partnerships where you can leverage each other's strengths. These approaches not only help you acquire properties with less money upfront but can also provide unique opportunities for appreciation and tax benefits that you might not have considered otherwise. The more creative you are with your financing, the more opportunities you'll discover to grow your real estate portfolio.

Ultimately, building a real estate network on a budget is about connecting with like-minded individuals who share your vision. Attend local meetups, join online forums, and engage with others passionate about real estate. By building relationships with experienced investors, you can learn about the nuances of appreciation and tax benefits while also discovering new strategies to enhance your investments. Remember, every great empire starts with a single step, and with the right knowledge and friendships, your dreams of creating a real estate empire are entirely within reach.

Chapter 19

Year 20 Breakthrough

Building a real estate empire

Real estate empire status

Building a real estate empire may sound like a distant dream, especially when you're just starting with a limited budget. However, the journey of three friends who decided to invest just twenty bucks a day proves that with determination and creativity, anything is possible. As they navigated the world of real estate, they discovered that success is not just about money; it's about teamwork, smart strategies, and a willingness to learn. Their story is a testament to the idea that anyone, no matter their financial status, can step into the world of real estate and thrive.

The friends began by pooling their resources, committing to save twenty dollars each day. This small amount might seem insignificant, but it laid the foundation for something much greater. They quickly realized that budgeting and disciplined saving were crucial. With their combined efforts, they started to build a fund that would allow them to explore investment opportunities. This initial commitment taught them the value of teamwork; each friend contributed not only financially but also with ideas and enthusiasm. Working together, they turned a simple savings plan into a launching pad for their ambitions.

As they ventured into the market, they learned about creative financing methods that would allow them to maximize their limited resources. They explored options like seller financing, where they could buy properties directly from owners without needing a bank. This approach opened doors that traditional financing methods might have closed. By thinking outside the box, they transformed their modest savings into legitimate investment opportunities. The friends discovered that innovation in financing could set them apart and provide them with an edge in the competitive real estate landscape.

Understanding the importance of property management, the trio adopted low-cost techniques to maintain and improve their investments. They took on the role of property managers themselves, learning about maintenance, tenant relations, and rental agreements. This hands-on experience not only saved them money but also gave them a deeper understanding of the real estate business. They found creative solutions to common problems, such as using social media to find tenants or organizing community events to foster good relations with their neighbors. Their proactive approach to property management became a cornerstone of their growing empire.

Networking played a vital role in their success. The friends quickly realized that building relationships with other investors, real estate agents, and mentors was essential. They attended local workshops and joined online forums, sharing their experiences and learning from others. By surrounding themselves with like-minded individuals, they gained valuable knowledge and access to exclusive opportunities. This supportive community encouraged them to dream bigger and take more calculated risks. Their journey illustrates that with the right mindset and a solid network, even the most modest beginnings can lead to a thriving real estate empire.

Financial freedom & early retirement

Financial freedom and early retirement may sound like dreams that only adults can achieve, but the truth is, with the right mindset and strategies, you can start laying the groundwork for these goals as a teenager. By leveraging your creativity, resourcefulness, and the support of friends, you can embark on a journey that leads to an empire built on real estate. Imagine waking up each day knowing that your investments are working for you, offering not just financial security but the freedom to pursue your passions and dreams.

The first step towards financial freedom is understanding the power of small investments. With just twenty dollars a day, you and your friends can begin pooling your resources to explore real estate opportunities. This doesn't mean you need to dive into expensive properties right away; instead, consider starting small by investing in low-cost properties or even exploring house hacking strategies. By renting out part of a property you own, you can cover your mortgage payments while living in a space you enjoy. This creative approach not only reduces living expenses but also accelerates your journey toward financial independence.

Cooperative investment strategies among friends can amplify your efforts significantly. When you work together, you can combine your strengths, share responsibilities, and mitigate risks. Forming a group allows you to leverage each member's unique skills, whether it's negotiating deals, managing properties, or handling finances. Together, you can create a powerful real estate network that opens doors to opportunities that would be challenging to tackle alone. The friendships you build along the way will not only make the process more enjoyable but also provide a support system that encourages growth and resilience.

Creative financing methods are essential tools in your arsenal as you navigate the real estate landscape. Explore options like seller financing, where the property owner allows you to pay in installments, or consider joint ventures that let you pool funds for larger investments. These strategies can help you acquire properties without needing a hefty down payment upfront. By educating yourselves on these techniques early on, you and your friends will be well-equipped to seize opportunities that others might overlook, setting the stage for a successful real estate career.

Finally, it's crucial to adopt a mindset that embraces learning and adaptability. The journey to financial freedom is filled with challenges, but seeing each obstacle as an opportunity can transform your experience. Engage in discussions, attend workshops, and build your knowledge base about property management techniques that are budget-friendly. Surrounding yourselves with mentors and peers who share your vision will inspire you to stay committed to your goals. Remember, achieving financial freedom and early retirement isn't just about the money; it's about creating a life that allows you to pursue what you love, all while knowing that your efforts today are paving the way for a brighter tomorrow.

Legacy planning and new ventures

Legacy planning is crucial, even for teenagers with dreams of building a real estate empire. It's not just about making quick profits today; it's about setting up a future that can benefit generations to come. As you embark on your journey with friends, consider how your actions now can create a lasting impact. Imagine the thrill of passing down investment properties to your kids or even a group of friends who share your passion. By thinking ahead and planning your legacy, you're not just creating wealth; you're building a foundation of success that can inspire others to follow in your footsteps.

When you dive into the world of real estate with your friends, it's essential to identify new ventures that align with your legacy goals. This could mean exploring properties that not only provide rental income but also contribute to community development. Look for opportunities to invest in up-and-coming neighborhoods or properties that can be transformed into affordable housing. These ventures can generate income while also leaving a positive mark on your community. Your choices today can pave the way for a brighter tomorrow, proving that real estate investment can be a powerful tool for social change.

Creative financing methods are your best friends when it comes to legacy planning. Instead of relying solely on traditional loans, think about how you can pool resources with your friends to invest in larger projects. Consider options like crowdfunding or partnering with local businesses to secure funding. These strategies not only make it easier to acquire properties but also foster a sense of teamwork and shared purpose. Each successful investment becomes a stepping stone toward a sustainable legacy, teaching you valuable lessons about collaboration and financial creativity along the way.

As you build your real estate network, remember that relationships are key to your legacy. Connect with mentors, join local real estate groups, and attend workshops to meet like-minded individuals. These connections can offer insights, resources, and even investment opportunities that you might not find on your own. Building a network isn't just about making contacts; it's about creating a community that supports your dreams. Each person you meet can play a role in your journey, and together you can create a ripple effect that extends far beyond your immediate circle.

Lastly, don't underestimate the power of house hacking and cooperative investment strategies. By pooling your resources with friends, you can invest in properties that might have seemed out of reach. Consider buying a multi-family home where you live in one unit and rent out the others. This not only helps cover your mortgage but also sets the stage for building a portfolio of investment properties. Every successful house hack can be a part of your legacy, teaching you and your friends the value of smart investing and teamwork. Remember, every dollar saved and every lesson learned is a step closer to the empire you dream of building together.

Chapter 20

The Wealth Blueprint for Readers

Replicating the Plan

How anyone can replicate the plan

Replicating the plan laid out in "Twenty Bucks and a Dream" is not just possible; it's an adventure waiting to unfold. Imagine gathering your closest friends, each armed with just $20 a day, and setting out on a journey to build something incredible together. The beauty of this approach lies in its simplicity and accessibility. You don't need a trust fund or a wealth of experience; all you need is a vision, a bit of creativity, and the willingness to work as a team. Every step you take can be a building block for your future, and by following the strategies outlined in this book, you can create your own real estate empire.

First, begin by forming a group of like-minded friends who share your ambition. This cooperative spirit is crucial. You're not just pooling resources; you're leveraging each other's strengths and ideas. Each member of the group brings unique skills to the table, whether it's research abilities, negotiation tactics, or financial know-how. By combining these talents, you can tackle challenges that may seem insurmountable when faced alone. Start by brainstorming your goals together, ensuring everyone is on the same page. This shared vision will fuel your determination and keep you motivated.

Next, dive into the world of budget real estate investing. Research properties that are undervalued or in need of some TLC. With a daily commitment of just $20 each, you can save up for down payments or repairs. Look for local workshops or online courses that teach the basics of real estate investing; many are free or low-cost. Use this knowledge to identify the best deals in your area. Remember, it's not about how much money you start with but how wisely you invest your limited resources. Be creative in your financing methods; consider options like seller financing or partnerships that can help you secure properties without a massive upfront investment.

Implementing low-cost property management techniques will also be vital as you grow your portfolio. You don't need to hire a property manager right away. Instead, divide responsibilities among your group. One friend can handle tenant communications, another can manage maintenance tasks, and someone else can keep track of finances. With smart organization and teamwork, you can effectively manage your properties while minimizing costs. This hands-on approach not only saves money but also gives you invaluable experience in running your real estate business.

Building a real estate network on a budget is another important step. Attend local real estate meetups, workshops, or networking events, even if they require a small fee. Connect with experienced investors and professionals willing to share their knowledge. Leverage social media platforms to join real estate groups where you can ask questions, seek advice, and find potential partners or mentors. Networking opens doors to opportunities you might not find on your own and can lead to collaborations that enhance your journey. Remember, every connection could be a stepping stone toward your dream.

Finally, consider house hacking as a way to maximize your investment potential. If you acquire a property, think about renting out rooms to help cover the mortgage. This strategy not only provides cash flow but also gives you real-world experience in property management and tenant relations. Encourage your group to develop creative solutions for maximizing income from your investments. As you work together, celebrate each success, no matter how small. Each step forward reinforces your bond and commitment to building something extraordinary. With determination, teamwork, and the strategies outlined in this book, anyone can replicate this plan and embark on their own journey toward a real estate empire.

Tools: savings tracker, deal calculator, equity use checklist

In the journey of building a real estate empire, especially with just twenty bucks a day, having the right tools can make all the difference. One of the most essential tools you can use is a savings tracker. This simple yet powerful tool allows you to monitor your progress as you save money toward your investment goals. Picture your savings tracker as a scoreboard in a game; it keeps you motivated and accountable. By breaking down your savings into smaller, manageable goals, you can celebrate each milestone, whether it's saving enough for your first down payment or funding renovations on a property you've acquired together.

Next on your toolkit is the deal calculator. This tool is crucial for anyone looking to make smart investment decisions. It helps you assess the potential profitability of a property by calculating important metrics such as cash flow, return on investment, and total expenses. With a deal calculator, you and your friends can evaluate various properties side by side, comparing their potential and making informed choices. This collaborative approach not only enhances your understanding of real estate investing but also strengthens the bond between you and your friends as you work toward a common goal.

Another indispensable resource is the equity use checklist. This checklist guides you through the process of leveraging the equity you build in your properties. By using equity wisely, you can fund new investments, renovations, or even pay down existing debts. Imagine the thrill of discovering that the value of your property has increased, allowing you to pull out some of that equity to reinvest in more properties. The equity use checklist not only helps you identify opportunities but also ensures you're making decisions that align with your long-term vision for your real estate empire.

As teenagers embarking on this adventure, it's essential to remember that these tools are not just about numbers; they represent dreams, teamwork, and the power of shared aspirations. Each time you input data into your savings tracker or analyze a potential deal with your calculator, you are taking steps toward your future. You are not just learning about real estate; you are gaining skills that will serve you throughout your life. Embrace the process, and let these tools empower you to turn your twenty bucks a day into a thriving real estate venture.

Ultimately, building a real estate empire is about more than just financial gain; it's about creating a legacy with your friends. By using your savings tracker, deal calculator, and equity use checklist, you are laying the foundation for a successful investment journey together. These tools will not only help you make informed decisions but will also foster communication and collaboration among your group. Remember, every step you take with these resources brings you closer to realizing your dreams, proving that with determination and the right strategies, you can accomplish incredible things, one property at a time.

Chapter 21

Real Estate Key Lessons

Common Pitfalls and How to Win

Mistakes to avoid

When embarking on the journey of building a real estate empire with just twenty bucks a day, it's essential to be aware of common pitfalls that can derail your dreams. One of the most significant mistakes to avoid is rushing into investments without doing thorough research. Many beginners are eager to make their first purchase and may overlook critical aspects such as market trends, property conditions, and neighborhood dynamics. Take the time to understand what makes a property a good investment. Gather information, analyze comparable sales, and consult with experienced investors. Knowledge will set you apart and empower you to make informed decisions, paving the way for lasting success.

Another common mistake is failing to communicate effectively with your friends and partners. Cooperative investment strategies rely heavily on trust and transparency. If one person in the group isn't on the same page regarding financial goals, risk tolerance, or property management methods, conflicts can arise. Regular meetings and open discussions are vital to aligning everyone's expectations and responsibilities. Create a structured approach to decision-making, and ensure that every member's voice is heard. This helps to strengthen your partnership and creates a solid foundation for your real estate endeavors.

Budgeting is a cornerstone of successful real estate investing, yet many young investors underestimate the importance of tracking expenses. A frequent mistake is overlooking the hidden costs associated with property ownership, such as maintenance, taxes, and insurance. It's crucial to develop a comprehensive budget that encompasses all potential expenses, allowing you to plan for both expected and unexpected costs. By being meticulous with your finances, you'll avoid unpleasant surprises that can jeopardize your investments and hinder your ability to reinvest profits.

Creative financing methods can open doors to opportunities that might seem out of reach, but relying solely on unconventional strategies without a solid understanding can lead to disaster. Many beginners mistakenly assume they can easily leverage techniques like seller financing or lease options without fully grasping their implications. It's vital to educate yourself about each method's risks and benefits before diving in. By doing so, you can confidently explore innovative financing solutions while minimizing the chances of making costly errors that could set you back in your journey.

Lastly, neglecting to build a real estate network on a budget can limit your growth potential. Many aspiring investors believe that networking is only for those with deep pockets, but that couldn't be further from the truth. Engaging with local real estate groups, attending meet-ups, and utilizing social media platforms can connect you with experienced mentors and like-minded individuals. By surrounding yourself with a supportive community, you can gain valuable insights, share resources, and even discover joint venture opportunities. Remember, real estate investing is not just about money; it's about collaboration and learning from those around you.

Success stories

In the journey of building a real estate empire, success stories illuminate the path for aspiring investors, especially teenagers eager to make their mark. Imagine three friends, each with a vision and a mere twenty bucks a day, coming together to turn their dreams into reality. They started out with small investments, pooling their resources and creativity to explore the world of real estate. Their story is a testament to the power of friendship, collaboration, and the belief that even the smallest contributions can lead to monumental achievements.

One of their first significant wins came from a low-cost house-hacking strategy. They found a neglected property in their neighborhood that was ripe for investment. By working together, they managed to secure the funds necessary for a down payment through their daily savings and creative financing methods they learned along the way. They transformed that property into a multi-unit rental space, allowing them to live in one unit while renting out the others. This not only covered their mortgage but also generated positive cash flow, proving that with teamwork and innovative thinking, young investors can turn a tight budget into a profitable venture.

Their success didn't stop there. Recognizing the importance of building a network, the trio attended local real estate meetups and workshops, often seeking out mentors who could guide them. They shared their story, learned from others, and built connections with fellow investors. This network opened doors to more opportunities, such as co-investing in larger projects and gaining access to valuable resources that would have otherwise been out of reach. Their willingness to learn and grow together became a cornerstone of their success, demonstrating how cooperative investment strategies can yield remarkable results.

As their investments began to flourish, they also embraced the idea of low-cost property management techniques. Rather than relying on expensive property managers, they took on the responsibility themselves. This experience taught them not only about managing tenants but also about maintaining properties efficiently. They became experts at finding cost-effective solutions for repairs and maintenance, which further increased their profitability. Their ability to adapt and innovate in property management showcased the potential for young investors to thrive without breaking the bank.

Ultimately, these friends' journey is an inspiring reminder that success in real estate is achievable, even on a limited budget. By combining their efforts, sharing knowledge, and embracing creative solutions, they built a robust real estate empire from just twenty bucks a day. Their story encourages teenagers everywhere to dream big and take action. With determination, collaboration, and an open mind, anyone can turn their aspirations into reality, proving that the future of real estate is bright for those willing to put in the work.

Tips from real estate professionals

When embarking on your real estate journey, learning from professionals can provide invaluable insights that set you on the right path. Real estate experts often emphasize the importance of education and continuous learning. Start by reading books, attending workshops, or even listening to podcasts that focus on real estate investing. Remember, knowledge is your most powerful tool. The more you know, the better equipped you'll be to make informed decisions. Don't hesitate to ask questions; successful investors love to share their stories and lessons learned, which can help you avoid common pitfalls.

One crucial tip from seasoned real estate professionals is to harness the power of networking, even on a budget. Building relationships with others in the industry can open doors to opportunities you might not find on your own. Attend local real estate meetups or join online forums where aspiring investors gather to exchange ideas. Surrounding yourself with like-minded peers can inspire creativity and collaboration, which is essential when pooling resources with friends. Remember, it's not just about what you know—who you know can significantly impact your investment journey.

Creative financing methods are another area where professionals can provide guidance. Many successful investors started with limited funds, so they understand the importance of thinking outside the box. Explore options like seller financing, where the property owner helps finance the purchase, or consider taking on a partner to share costs. Don't shy away from using your negotiation skills; sometimes, a simple conversation can lead to better terms that make a deal more feasible. Creativity in financing can be the difference between a missed opportunity and a successful investment.

Property management is often seen as a daunting task, but professionals advise that it doesn't have to break the bank. Low-cost property management techniques can save you time and money. For instance, consider self-management for your first few properties. This not only helps you understand the ins and outs of property management but also keeps expenses low. Use technology to your advantage; there are numerous apps and software that can simplify tenant communication, rent collection, and maintenance requests, allowing you to manage your investments efficiently without high costs.

Finally, house hacking is a strategy that professionals often recommend, particularly for those just starting out. By renting out a portion of your home or investing in multi-family properties, you can significantly reduce your living expenses while building equity. This approach not only helps you cover mortgage payments but also provides practical experience in managing tenants. Remember, every small step you take can lead to bigger successes. By embracing these tips from real estate professionals, you and your friends can transform your $20 a day into a thriving real estate empire, one smart decision at a time.

Chapter 22

Scaling Up Your Empire

Planning for Future Investments

Planning for Future Investments

Planning for future investments is essential, especially when you're starting with a modest budget like twenty bucks a day. As teenagers with dreams of building a real estate empire, it's crucial that you think ahead and set clear goals. Imagine how exciting it will be to look back and see how your investments have grown over time! Start by discussing your aspirations with your friends, as having a shared vision can motivate you all to stay committed. Create a vision board or a digital document that outlines your investment goals, whether they involve purchasing your first property, saving for renovations, or contributing to a larger project together.

Next, consider the power of cooperative investment strategies among friends. Pooling resources can significantly amplify your purchasing power, allowing you to access opportunities that might be out of reach for an individual. Set up regular meetings to discuss potential investments, share research, and analyze market trends. This collaborative approach not only fosters teamwork but also encourages each member to contribute their unique skills and knowledge, creating a well-rounded investment strategy. Remember, the more you learn together, the stronger your foundation will be for making informed decisions in the future.

As you plan for future investments, don't overlook the creative financing methods available to you. Traditional bank loans might not be feasible for everyone, but there are many other ways to fund your ventures. Explore options like seller financing, where the property seller allows you to make payments over time, or consider crowdfunding platforms that cater to real estate. These alternative financing methods can open doors to properties and investments that fit your budget. Embrace the challenge of thinking outside the box, and encourage your friends to brainstorm together about innovative funding solutions.

Low-cost property management techniques will also play a crucial role in your investment journey. Once you acquire properties, you'll want to ensure they are managed efficiently without draining your funds. Learn about DIY maintenance, using technology to streamline processes, and leveraging your network for help. For example, if one of your friends has a knack for handyman work, have them take charge of small repairs. By minimizing costs and maximizing efficiency, you'll be better equipped to reinvest profits into future projects, propelling your real estate aspirations forward.

Lastly, building a real estate network on a budget is vital for your long-term success. Attend local meetups, join online forums, and engage with real estate groups on social media. Networking can lead to mentorship opportunities, partnerships, and valuable insights into the market. Share what you learn with your friends and encourage them to do the same. Remember, every connection you make can potentially open new doors for investment opportunities. By actively cultivating relationships within the real estate community, you'll be better positioned to navigate the landscape and achieve your dreams of building a thriving real estate empire together.

Expanding Your Network and Knowledge

Expanding your network and knowledge is crucial in the journey of building a real estate empire, especially when you're just starting with limited resources. As teenagers, you possess an incredible advantage: your enthusiasm and openness to learn. Surrounding yourself with like-minded individuals can ignite new ideas and provide support that propels your journey forward. Attend local workshops, join online forums, or participate in community events focused on real estate. The relationships you build now will not only enrich your understanding but can also lead to collaborative opportunities that can amplify your investment potential.

One of the most effective ways to expand your knowledge is through mentorship. Seek out experienced investors who can guide you through the complexities of real estate. They have walked the path you are just beginning to explore and can share invaluable insights that textbooks often overlook. Don't hesitate to reach out—most successful professionals are eager to help the next generation find their footing. Remember, every expert was once a beginner, and having someone to turn to for advice can make all the difference in your journey.

Another powerful strategy is to leverage online resources. The internet is a treasure trove of information, from podcasts and webinars to blogs and social media groups dedicated to real estate. Engage with content that addresses budget-friendly investing and cooperative investment strategies among friends. You can learn about creative financing methods, low-cost property management techniques, and even house hacking tips that align with your goals. The more you educate yourself, the more confident you will become in making informed decisions.

As you expand your network, think creatively about how to collaborate with your friends. Form study groups to analyze potential properties or pool your resources to invest together. This approach not only reduces individual financial burden but also fosters teamwork and strengthens your relationships. Encourage open discussions about your goals, challenges, and successes. This collective effort can lead to innovative solutions that might not have been considered individually, and it will prepare you all for future challenges in the real estate world.

Ultimately, expanding your network and knowledge is about building a community that supports and inspires you. The connections you make today can turn into partnerships that last a lifetime. Embrace every opportunity to learn and grow, and don't be afraid to step outside of your comfort zone. With determination and collaboration, you and your friends can turn that initial twenty bucks a day into an empire that not only fulfills your dreams but also creates lasting impacts for others in your community.

Inspiring Others to Join You

In the journey of building a real estate empire, the most powerful tool you have is not just knowledge or money, but the ability to inspire others. When you share your vision and enthusiasm with your friends, you create a ripple effect that can turn dreams into reality. Imagine gathering your closest pals and igniting their interest in real estate. By sharing stories of potential success and illustrating how just twenty bucks a day can lead to fantastic opportunities, you can instill a sense of excitement and purpose. This enthusiasm can transform a simple idea into a shared dream, motivating everyone to take action together.

Inspiring others is about more than just the financial gains; it's about creating a community of support and shared aspirations. When you invite friends to join you in your real estate journey, you are fostering an environment where everyone can learn and grow together. Each person brings unique skills and perspectives that can contribute to your collective success. Whether it's a knack for finding undervalued properties, a talent for negotiation, or an eye for design, pooling resources and talents can lead to innovative solutions and strategies that you might not have thought of alone.

To effectively inspire your friends, storytelling can be a powerful tool. Share your vision of what you want to achieve in real estate and paint a vivid picture of the lifestyle and freedom it can provide. Talk about how house hacking can help reduce living expenses, or how cooperative investment strategies can make owning property more accessible. When your friends see real-life examples of success, it becomes easier for them to envision themselves in similar situations. This connection between your dreams and their potential can ignite a passion for real estate that turns passive interest into active participation.

As you gather your friends and embark on this exciting venture, encourage open communication and collaboration. Hold brainstorming sessions where everyone can contribute ideas and express concerns. Create a culture of support where questions are welcomed, and learning from mistakes is encouraged. By fostering an environment where everyone feels valued, you empower your friends to take ownership of their roles in the group. This sense of belonging not only strengthens your bond but also enhances your collective ability to navigate challenges and celebrate victories together.

Finally, remember that inspiring others is an ongoing process. Celebrate every small victory along the way, whether it's saving enough for a down payment or finding a great deal on a property. Acknowledge the hard work and dedication of your friends, and continuously share your vision to keep the momentum going. As your real estate empire grows, so will the impact you have on those around you. By inspiring others to join you in your journey, you're not just building wealth; you're creating a legacy of collaboration, empowerment, and shared dreams for generations to come.

Chapter 23

The Journey Ahead

Reflecting on Your Accomplishments

Reflecting on Your Accomplishments

Reflecting on your accomplishments is an essential step in any journey, especially when that journey involves building something as ambitious as a real estate empire with your friends. As teenagers embarking on this adventure, it's important to pause and acknowledge how far you've come, even if your starting point was just twenty bucks a day. Each small victory, whether it's securing your first property or successfully budgeting your funds, deserves recognition. These moments are the building blocks of your future successes and can inspire you to push forward even when challenges arise.

Consider the moments when you pooled your resources with your friends, transforming those twenty dollars into opportunities. Each decision you made collectively, from researching potential properties to discussing financing options, was a step toward your dream. Reflecting on these accomplishments helps solidify your confidence and reminds you that teamwork and collaboration can lead to extraordinary results. Celebrate the times you brainstormed creative financing methods or found innovative ways to manage properties on a budget. These experiences not only enhance your skills but also deepen your friendships, creating a solid foundation for your real estate empire.

As you look back, think about the lessons learned along the way. Every setback you faced, whether it was a deal that didn't go as planned or a property that required more work than expected, taught you invaluable lessons about resilience, patience, and adaptability. These experiences will shape your future decisions and strategies. Embrace the growth that comes from reflecting on both your successes and challenges. Each lesson learned is a stepping stone that prepares you for the next phase of your journey in real estate investing.

Moreover, reflecting on your accomplishments can help you visualize your future goals. Take the time to create a vision board or a written list of where you want to be in the next few years. Incorporating your past achievements into this vision can serve as motivation. When you see how far you've come, it reinforces your belief in what's possible. As you dream bigger, remember that each goal is achievable when you have a supportive network of friends by your side, and that your journey is just as important as the destination.

Finally, sharing your accomplishments with others can amplify their significance. Whether it's discussing your journey with peers, mentors, or even on social media, sharing your story can inspire others to embark on their own paths. It reinforces the idea that success is not just about the end result but the journey you take to get there. Your experiences may motivate other teenagers to collaborate, invest, and dream big, just like you and your friends. Reflecting on your accomplishments not only empowers you but also creates a ripple effect that can lead others to build their own real estate empires.

Setting New Goals

Setting new goals is an essential part of your journey in building a real estate empire, especially when you're starting with just twenty bucks a day. As teenagers, you have the unique advantage of time and energy, allowing you to set ambitious objectives that can shape your future. The key is to define what you want to achieve, whether that's saving enough for your first investment property, mastering budget-friendly investment strategies, or learning the ins and outs of cooperative investment with your friends. Visualizing your goals will help you stay motivated and focused on the path ahead.

Begin by breaking down your larger aspirations into smaller, manageable goals. If your dream is to own several rental properties by the time you're in your twenties, set milestones for yourself. Perhaps your first goal could be saving a specific amount each month. From there, focus on learning about low-cost property management techniques or house hacking strategies. Each small victory will build your confidence and keep you engaged in the process. Remember, each dollar saved and each lesson learned is a step closer to turning your dreams into reality.

Involving your friends in this journey can amplify your success. As you set new goals, consider how you can collaborate with your friends to achieve them together. Share your aspirations and hold each other accountable. You might decide to pool your resources to invest in a property that none of you could afford individually. Collaborative investment strategies not only make real estate more accessible but also deepen your friendships. Working together towards a common goal can lead to creative solutions and innovative ideas that you may not have considered alone.

Don't shy away from thinking creatively about financing your investments. Setting goals in this area means exploring unconventional methods, such as leveraging crowdfunding platforms or finding local investors interested in joining your venture. Challenge yourself to think outside the box—perhaps you could offer to manage a property in exchange for a percentage of the profits, or even partner with someone who has capital but lacks the time to invest. These creative financing methods can open doors that you never thought possible, allowing you to reach your goals more quickly.

Finally, the importance of building a real estate network on a budget cannot be overstated. Attend local meetups, engage with online forums, and connect with mentors willing to share their experiences. Setting goals in this area means actively seeking out relationships that can provide guidance and support. Each connection you make can lead to new opportunities, insights, and partnerships that will propel you further along your real estate journey. Embrace the power of networking, and you will find that your dreams are not just possible but within reach.

The Future of Your Real Estate Empire

The future of your real estate empire is not just a distant dream; it's a tangible goal that can be achieved with creativity, collaboration, and a strong vision. As teenagers, you are at a unique advantage. You have the energy, the passion, and the willingness to take risks that can lead to incredible opportunities. Imagine pooling together your resources, even if it's just twenty bucks a day, and watching that initial investment grow into a thriving real estate portfolio. Your journey may not follow a traditional path, but the excitement of building something significant with your friends will be the driving force behind your success.

As you embark on this adventure, embrace the power of cooperative investment strategies. Working alongside friends means you can share not only the financial burden but also the workload, ideas, and responsibilities. Each of you brings unique skills and perspectives to the table, whether it's budgeting, negotiating, or marketing. By collaborating and leveraging your strengths, you can tackle challenges head-on and find creative solutions that individual investments might not allow. Remember, the best empires are built on a foundation of teamwork and trust.

Creative financing methods are your best friends in this journey. As budding entrepreneurs, think outside the box and explore options like seller financing, lease options, or even crowdfunding. These methods can help you acquire properties without needing a mountain of cash upfront. With your collective vision, you can negotiate deals that align with your budget while maximizing potential returns. Stay informed about emerging trends, and don't be afraid to pitch your ideas to potential investors or mentors who might see the value in your vision.

Managing properties effectively is crucial for sustaining your real estate empire, especially on a budget. Low-cost property management techniques can save you money while ensuring your investments continue to thrive. Consider using technology to streamline your operations, from tenant communication to maintenance requests. By keeping overhead costs low, you can reinvest profits back into your empire, allowing it to grow even further. Plus, mastering these skills early on will set you apart as reliable and savvy investors in the future.

Building a real estate network on a budget may seem daunting, but it's a vital component of your empire's success. Attend local meetups, engage with online forums, and seek out mentors who can provide guidance and support. Surrounding yourself with like-minded individuals can lead to partnerships, new ideas, and valuable advice. Share your journey with others, and don't hesitate to ask for help when needed. Remember, each connection you make can open doors to new opportunities, propelling your real estate empire into a bright and prosperous future.

Chapter 24

Why Most People Stay Poor

And How Not To

The old Toyota Corolla pulled into the office parking lot, taking its usual spot near the back entrance. From it emerged Richard Coleman, dressed in a neatly pressed but slightly outdated suit. His colleagues at the accounting firm nodded politely as they passed him on their way inside, some climbing out of BMWs and Audis that gleamed in the morning sun.

For ten years, Richard had endured good-natured ribbing about his car. "When are you going to upgrade that thing, Rich?" they'd ask. "You're a senior accountant now—treat yourself!" What his colleagues didn't know was that Richard's net worth had recently crossed the $1.2 million mark. While they were financing luxury vehicles and struggling with credit card debt, Richard had been quietly building wealth through consistent $20 daily investments and strategic real estate acquisitions. "I could buy any car in this parking lot with cash," Richard told me, smiling. "But that's exactly why I don't." Richard understood something fundamental that his higher-spending colleagues didn't: The path to wealth isn't paved with impressive purchases—it's built through unremarkable daily decisions that prioritize tomorrow over today.

The Invisible Epidemic: Financial Illusion

In America today, we face an epidemic more pervasive than any virus: the illusion of wealth. We see it everywhere—the colleague with the luxury car, the friend with the lavish vacation photos on social media, the neighbor who just renovated their entire home. These visible displays create the impression of wealth, but they often mask a troubling reality: negative net worth, crushing debt, and financial fragility.

Consider these statistics:

- 78% of American workers live paycheck to paycheck
- The average household carries $7,951 in credit card debt
- 45% of Americans have nothing saved for retirement
- 40% of adults couldn't cover a $400 emergency without borrowing

Yet simultaneously, we're surrounded by displays of apparent prosperity. This contradiction creates what psychologists call "pluralistic ignorance"—a situation where people privately reject a norm but publicly uphold it because they incorrectly assume everyone else accepts it. In simpler terms: everyone's faking it, because they think everyone else is making it.

The Four Wealth Traps

Through my research with hundreds of individuals—both those who built wealth and those who didn't—I've identified four primary traps that keep most people financially stagnant. Understanding these traps is the first step to avoiding them.

Wealth Trap #1: The Income Illusion

"If I just made more money, my financial problems would disappear."This belief is perhaps the most pervasive and destructive financial myth in modern society. It's also demonstrably false. Consider professional athletes who make millions yet file for bankruptcy shortly after retirement. Or lottery winners who end up worse off than before their windfall. Or the countless high-income professionals living paycheck to paycheck despite six-figure salaries.

Michael, one of our three friends from Chapter 1, experienced this firsthand after receiving a significant promotion at his school."When my salary jumped from $46,000 to $62,000, I was ecstatic," he recalls. "I thought all my money problems were solved. But six months later, I was still just as financially stressed—I had just upgraded my problems."His rent increased when he moved to a nicer apartment. He ate out more frequently. He bought a better car with a higher payment. His lifestyle expanded to consume his additional income, leaving him no better off financially.This is what economists call "lifestyle inflation," and it's the primary reason increased income rarely translates to increased wealth.

The truth is simple but difficult to accept: *Wealth is not determined by how much you make, but by how much you keep.*

A teacher saving $20 a day will outperform a doctor spending every penny of their substantial income. Income matters only to the extent that it creates gap between earnings and spending—what financial experts call your "savings rate ."This fundamental truth—that income without saving creates only an illusion of wealth—is why our $20 wealth formula works regardless of your earnings. It focuses not on making more, but on keeping more of what you make.

Wealth Trap #2: The Consumption Identity

"I work hard, so I deserve nice things."

"This purchase shows I've 'made it.'"

"You can't take it with you when you die."

These justifications for consumption are so common they've become cultural mantras. They reflect a deeper psychological trap: tying our identity and self-worth to our consumption habits. Sarah encountered this trap through her work as a graphic designer, where she was surrounded by colleagues who showcased their success through visible consumption."I felt intense pressure to look successful," she admits. "I'd show up to client meetings and everyone had designer bags, expensive watches, and the latest tech. I started believing I needed these things to be taken seriously." This led to what she calls her "fake rich phase," during which she spent money she didn't have on things she didn't need to impress people she didn't even like. The turning point came when she calculated the true cost of these purchases. A $2,500 designer bag represented 125 days of her $20 wealth contribution. That single purchase was potentially worth tens of thousands in future wealth. "Once I started thinking in terms of 'future dollars' rather than 'today dollars,' my perspective completely changed," she explains. This shift—from consumption identity to investor identity—marks a crucial psychological transformation on the path to wealth. Those who remain trapped in consumption identity will forever confuse the appearance of wealth with actual wealth. They purchase depreciating assets that signal prosperity while simultaneously preventing them from achieving it.Meanwhile, those who develop an investor identity derive satisfaction not from what they display, but from what they build. Their self-worth becomes tied not to visible consumption but to invisible growth.

Wealth Trap #3: The Now vs. Later Dilemma

Imagine I offered you a choice: $100 today or $150 one year from now. Which would you choose? Research shows most people would take the $100 today, even though waiting would yield a 50% return—far more than any reasonable investment could provide.This preference for immediate rewards over larger future benefits is called "temporal discounting," and it's a fundamental aspect of human psychology. Our brains are wired to prioritize immediate gratification over future benefits. Tom struggled with this extensively before beginning his wealth journey."I knew intellectually that saving was important," he explains. "But when Friday came around and friends were heading out, the abstract idea of 'future wealth' couldn't compete with the concrete reality of having fun today."

His solution? Making the future concrete.

Tom created detailed visualizations of his future wealthy self. He wrote letters from his "future self" describing the freedom and opportunities that financial independence would provide. He calculated exactly how much today's sacrifices would be worth in 10 and 20 years. "I had to make my future self as real as my present self," he says. "Once I did that, saying no to unnecessary expenses became easier. It wasn't deprivation—it was a choice between giving $20 to a restaurant today or giving thousands to my future self."This psychological technique—making the future tangible—is critical to overcoming our innate bias toward immediate gratification.

Wealth Trap #4: The Solo Mindset

"I have to figure this out on my own."

"I don't know enough to start investing."

"Rich people know secrets that I don't."

These beliefs reflect the final major wealth trap: the solo mindset—the belief that wealth building is a solitary journey that requires rare knowledge or exceptional capabilities. The reality is precisely the opposite. Wealth building is most successful as a collaborative endeavor supported by shared knowledge and mutual accountability. This insight was perhaps the most crucial factor in the success of our three friends. By pooling their resources, they reached critical investment thresholds more quickly. By combining their skills, they covered each other's knowledge gaps. And by providing mutual accountability, they maintained consistency during difficult periods." There were definitely times I would have given up if I was doing this alone," admits Sarah. "Like the month our first property needed an expensive plumbing repair right when my car broke down. I was ready to pull my money out and stop the whole experiment."

It was Tom who talked her through this crisis, reminding her of their long-term vision and helping her find alternative solutions to her immediate cash flow problem. This collaborative approach doesn't mean you need partners to invest with (though that can be advantageous). It simply means rejecting the myth that wealth building requires rare genius or must be pursued in isolation.

The most successful wealth builders leverage:

- Communities of like-minded individuals
- Mentors who have already achieved what they seek
- Professional advisors in specific domains
- Investment partners who bring complementary skills
- Accountability relationships that maintain consistency

These connections provide knowledge, perspective, motivation, and resilience that are simply unavailable to the solo wealth-builder.

Breaking Free: The Wealth Mindset Transformation

Understanding these four wealth traps is necessary but not sufficient. To build extraordinary wealth from ordinary income, you must actively transform your financial psychology. Here are the five critical mindset shifts that enabled Sarah, Tom, Michael, and countless others to escape these traps and build sustainable wealth:

Mindset Shift #1: From Consumer to Producer

The average American sees money primarily as a means to consume. The wealth builder sees money as a tool to produce. This fundamental shift changes everything. Instead of asking "What can I buy with this money?" the wealth-minded person asks "What can this money produce for me?"A simple mental exercise: Before any significant purchase, calculate how much that money could generate if invested instead:

- A $35,000 car could instead generate approximately $175,000 over 20 years if invested in income-producing assets

- A $5 daily coffee habit represents approximately $182,000 in missed wealth over 20 years

- A $2,000 vacation could instead grow to $10,000 over 20 years

This doesn't mean never enjoying purchases or experiences. It simply means making these decisions with full awareness of their true long-term cost."I still take vacations and buy things I enjoy," Michael explains. "But I make these decisions consciously, understanding exactly what I'm trading for these experiences."

Mindset Shift #2: From Status to Stealth

Wealth builders understand that displaying wealth and building wealth are often mutually exclusive activities."I drive a used Honda with 150,000 miles on it," Tom told me. "My colleagues think I'm broke. Meanwhile, I own 19 rental properties and have a seven-figure net worth." This "stealth wealth" approach isn't about deprivation—it's about prioritization. By rejecting the social pressure to display success through consumption, wealth builders redirect those resources toward assets that actually create wealth.This shift requires security in your self-worth and the courage to resist social comparison. It means finding satisfaction in knowing your financial truth rather than in displaying a financial facade.

Mindset Shift #3: From Scarcity to Abundance

Those trapped in financial stagnation often operate from a scarcity mindset—a belief that resources are limited and must be jealously guarded. This leads to fear-based financial decisions and resistance to investment opportunities. Wealth builders, conversely, operate from an abundance perspective. They see money as a renewable resource that can be cultivated and grown. This doesn't mean reckless optimism, but rather a fundamental belief in the possibility of expansion rather than the inevitability of limitation. "When we started, I was terrified of running out of money," Sarah admits. "Every dollar I put into our investment fund felt like a dollar I might desperately need later. But gradually I realized that money deployed strategically doesn't disappear—it multiplies."This shift from scarcity to abundance enables the consistent investment necessary for long-term wealth building.

Mindset Shift #4: From Short-Term to Long-Term

“The wealthy think in decades. The poor think in days”- Justice S.M Prosperity .

This extended time horizon fundamentally changes how financial decisions are evaluated. Small sacrifices become meaningful investments. Temporary setbacks become learning opportunities rather than catastrophes. Market fluctuations become irrelevant against the backdrop of long-term trends. "I stopped watching our properties' values daily or even monthly," Michael explains. "I began thinking about where they'd be in 10 or 20 years instead. This completely eliminated the stress of short-term volatility." This long-term perspective provides both psychological resilience and strategic advantage. While others react emotionally to market movements, the long-term investor remains steadily focused on proven wealth-building principles.

Mindset Shift #5: From Solo to Synergy

Finally, wealth builders recognize that financial success accelerates through collaboration. They actively seek knowledge, partnerships, and support rather than trying to master every aspect of wealth building alone."Our individual $20 daily contributions weren't impressive," Tom says. "But combined, they gave us the critical mass to start investing meaningfully. And our different skills complemented each other perfectly—Sarah's eye for good properties, my negotiation abilities, Michael's organizational skills."This collaborative mindset extends beyond direct investment partnerships to include building a network of mentors, advisors, and fellow wealth builders who provide support, knowledge, and accountability.

The Wealth Psychology Assessment

Before proceeding to the practical aspects of the $20 wealth formula, it's essential to understand your current financial psychology. The assessment below will help identify which wealth traps most affect you and which mindset shifts require your greatest attention.

For each statement, rate yourself from 1 (strongly disagree) to 5 (strongly agree):

<u>**Income Illusion Assessment:**</u>

1. I believe increasing my income is the primary solution to my financial challenges
2. When I receive additional money (bonus, raise, etc.), I typically spend more
3. I know exactly what percentage of my income I save each month
4. I focus more on earning than on optimizing my spending

<u>**Consumption Identity Assessment:**</u>

1. I sometimes purchase things to impress others or signal success
2. I justify luxury purchases as "rewards" for hard work
3. My possessions are an important part of how I see myself
4. I feel pressure to maintain a certain lifestyle based on my social circle or career

<u>**Now vs. Later Assessment:**</u>

1. I find it difficult to save for long-term goals
2. Immediate expenses usually take priority over saving/investing
3. I have a clear vision of my financial future in 10+ years
4. I regularly consider how current spending affects my future wealth

Solo Mindset Assessment:

1. I feel I should figure out financial matters independently
2. I'm hesitant to discuss money or investments with others
3. I actively seek financial knowledge from various sources
4. I have people in my life who share my wealth-building goals

Scoring Guide:

For each category, add your scores (reversing scores for questions 3 and 4, where 1=5, 2=4, etc.)

- 16-20: High vulnerability to this wealth trap
- 11-15: Moderate vulnerability
- 6-10: Low vulnerability
- 4-5: Strength in this area

Understanding your psychological starting point will help you apply the $20 wealth formula more effectively. The areas where you scored highest represent your priority areas for mindset transformation.

From Psychology to Action

In the chapters that follow, we'll move from the psychological foundation to the practical implementation of the $20 wealth formula. But remember: the mindset shifts described in this chapter are not merely preliminary—they are ongoing requirements for wealth-building success. As you progress through your wealth journey, regularly revisit these concepts. Financial psychology isn't something you solve once and for all—it's a continuous practice that evolves as your wealth grows. Richard Coleman—the accountant with the old Toyota and the seven-figure net worth—put it this way: "Building wealth isn't primarily about understanding money. It's about understanding yourself. Once you master your financial psychology, the practical aspects become almost automatic." In the next chapter, we'll explore how to leverage your daily $20 contributions to acquire your first real estate investment—the foundational asset that will begin your journey to millions. But first, take time to complete the Wealth Psychology Assessment. Identify which wealth traps have been holding you back and which mindset shifts will be most crucial to your success. Remember: Wealth building begins not in your bank account, but in your mind.

****Action Steps:****

1. Complete the Wealth Psychology Assessment
2. Identify your primary wealth trap(s)
3. Select one mindset shift to focus on this week
4. Find an accountability partner to discuss these concepts with
5. Write a letter from your "future wealthy self" to your present self, describing the benefits of your wealth-building journey

The path from $20 a day to millions begins with these psychological foundations. Master them, and the practical steps that follow will become not just possible, but inevitable.

Chapter 25

Prayers and Declarations for Financial Growth

Prayers for wisdom, opportunity, and discipline

Daily/weekly prayers for wisdom, opportunity, and discipline

In the journey of building a real estate empire, the power of daily and weekly prayers can be a guiding light. As teenagers embarking on this exciting adventure with friends, embracing the practice of prayer can help you cultivate wisdom, discern opportunities, and strengthen your resolve for discipline. Each morning, take a moment to reflect and ask for guidance in your endeavors. A simple prayer for wisdom can open your mind to innovative ideas and strategies that you might not have considered before. This daily ritual can help you align your goals with your values and encourage you to think creatively about how to make the most out of your limited resources.

As you gather with your friends, turn your weekly meet-ups into a time of reflection and prayer. Share your aspirations and challenges, and collectively pray for opportunities to arise in your real estate journey. When you ask for opportunities, focus on being open to the unexpected. Perhaps it's a property listing that pops up, or a networking event that leads to a valuable connection. By inviting your friends to join in this practice, you create a shared sense of purpose and encouragement that can lift everyone's spirits and keep your dreams alive.

Discipline is key in any investment strategy, especially when starting with limited funds. Incorporate a prayer for discipline into your routine to help you stay committed to your goals. It can be easy to get distracted by the allure of quick wins or the excitement of new ventures, but prayer can serve as a reminder of why you started this journey in the first place. Developing the discipline to stick to your budget, evaluate deals carefully, and invest time in learning will set you apart as you navigate the real estate landscape.

Additionally, prayer can foster a strong sense of community among you and your friends. By encouraging open discussions about your hopes and fears, you reinforce your bond and create an environment where everyone feels supported. This solidarity will be invaluable when you face challenges or setbacks, reminding you that you are not alone in your quest. As you pray together, you'll strengthen your commitment to one another and your shared vision of building a successful real estate empire.

Ultimately, the combination of daily and weekly prayers for wisdom, opportunity, and discipline can serve as a powerful foundation for your real estate investing journey. Embrace this practice not just as a ritual, but as a means to cultivate a mindset that thrives on collaboration and creativity. With each prayer, you'll find that your aspirations become clearer, your resolve grows stronger, and your path to success becomes illuminated. Together, with faith and dedication, you and your friends can turn your twenty bucks a day into a thriving real estate empire.

www.ingramcontent.com/pod-product-compliance
Lightning Source LLC
LaVergne TN
LVHW050917210926
848482LV00012B/478
* 9 7 9 8 3 4 9 3 3 7 2 3 9 *